# GET MORE ~~OUT OF YOUR~~
# MARCO POLO GUIDE

IT'S AS SIMPLE AS THIS

**1** go.marco-polo.com/ham

**2** download and discover

# GO!

WORKS OFFLINE!

**SYMBOLE**

| | |
|---|---|
| INSIDER TIP | Insider Tip |
| ★ | Highlight |
| ⬤⬤⬤⬤ | Best of ... |
| 🔆 | Scenic view |
| ♻ | Responsible travel: fair trade principles and the environment respected |
| (\*) | Telephone numbers that are not toll-free |

**PRICE CATEGORIES
HOTELS**

| | |
|---|---|
| *Expensive* | over 180 euros |
| *Moderate* | 120–180 euros |
| *Budget* | under 120 euros |

The prices are for two people
in a double room per night
including breakfast

**PRICE CATEGORIES
RESTAURANTS**

| | |
|---|---|
| *Expensive* | over 25 euros |
| *Moderate* | 15–25 euros |
| *Budget* | under 15 euros |

Prices are for an average
main dish without drinks

# CONTENTS

---

**MAPS IN THE GUIDEBOOK**
(132 A1) Page numbers and
coordinates refer to the street
atlas and the map of Hamburg
and the surrounding area on
p. 150/151
(0) Site/address located off the
map
Coordinates are also given for
places that are not marked on
the street atlas

(🛱 A–B 2–3) Refers to the
removable pull-out map

**INSIDE FRONT COVER:**
The best Highlights

**INSIDE BACK COVER:**
Public transportation
route map

# The best MARCO POLO Insider Tips

## Our top 15 Insider Tips

**INSIDER TIP** **Chic and colourful**

With its many old buildings, maze of streets, squares, shops, traditional pubs and hip hangouts, *Ottensen* is one of Hamburg's most popular districts → **p. 51**

**INSIDER TIP** **Meese meets visitors**

Jonathan Meese's eccentric artistic creations can be admired in the galleries of the *Sammlung Falckenberg* in Harburg – by prior arrangement only, but it is well worth it → **p. 58**

**INSIDER TIP** **A bit of an oddity**

Punks, mothers and canvassers with clipboards all congregate here at *Park Fiction* in St Pauli under plastic palm trees to play basketball or have a beer (photo right) → **p. 40**

**INSIDER TIP** **View from the bunker**

The view from the *Energiebunker* extends well beyond the Elbe island of Wilhelmsburg. There's coffee and cake on the terrace and information on the concept of generating environmental-friendly energy → **p. 115**

**INSIDER TIP** **Cakes to die for**

The whole Schanzenviertel is a trendy area, but the *Herr Max* café outdoes them all: cakes and petits fours decorated with grinning skulls or skeletons – they look amazing and they're also delicious → **p. 62**

**INSIDER TIP** **Tasty fish!**

By the entrance to the Alter Elbtunnel is *Käpt'n Schwarz* which sells delicious fish rolls! Check out the onion slicing machine! → **p. 64**

**INSIDER TIP** **One time around**

With the bright red boats of the *Maritime Circle Line* you can travel across the harbour to the former 'emigration port' of Ballinstadt → **p. 57**

**INSIDER TIP** **Lunch break at Bodo's**

Sink into a deckchair at *Bodo's Bootssteg* on the Alster – that's the life. And afterwards you can always hire a rowing boat → **p. 62**

### INSIDER TIP Culture in the attic

The *Nachtasyl* at the well-regarded Thalia-Theater, high up in the roof of the old building on Gerhart-Hauptmann-Platz, is one of Hamburg's trendiest bars with a regular programme of live shows → **p. 88**

### INSIDER TIP Friendly walruses

They mess around, grunting and snorting into their hairy moustaches, and they are more entertaining than any YouTube video: the walruses in the *Tierpark Hagenbeck* zoo even hold out their flippers for the keepers who feed them daily with squid → **p. 116**

### INSIDER TIP Beach with a harbour view

*Strandpauli*, the original rock of Hamburg beach clubs is still located where it was first established. There is a fantastic view of the shops and docks; salsa dance classes in summer, and in winter-time a cheese fondue in the wooden chalet → **p. 83**

### INSIDER TIP Seaman's pub with TV experience

The *Schellfischposten* at the Fischmarkt is experiencing something of a revival thanks to Ina Müller's TV show *'Ina's Nacht'*; but there's always something going on, even without cameras → **p. 87**

### INSIDER TIP Get grooving at Fischmarkt

At *Golem* the drum kit rests on Persian rugs and Hamburg's jazz musicians take centre stage for late night sessions. *Fatjazz* is the city's best music ensemble → **p. 83**

### INSIDER TIP Beam me up, Scotty!

Take a seat and become a stargazer! The brand-new refurbished *Planetarium* is one of the world's state-of-the-art venues (photo left) → **p. 58**

### INSIDER TIP Hammonia forever

They are not just beautiful, but age well too. The 'Hamburg bag' from the traditional luggage and bag shop *Klockmann* at the *Gänsemarkt* (goose market) → **p. 78**

# BEST OF ...

**FOR FREE**

● *To the bridge!*
It's actually only an office building, but you can go up onto the roof of the *Dockland* for free, from where you'll have a view of the Elbe like the captain does from his bridge – spectacular! → p. 50

● *Face to face with Antje*
Once the mascot of the local broadcasting company, today the walrus (which is now stuffed) greets visitors young and old to the *Zoologische Sammlung der Universität* (the university's zoological collection) in Grindel – along with tigers, bears and wildebeest. And all that for free ... → p. 117

● *Hafencity at a glance*
The *Infocenter Kesselhaus* not only has a gigantic model of the city and Hafencity, but also lots of interactive information about living in the city – architecture, urban expansion – everything about the future of Hamburg. The centre also runs free tours through Hafencity on weekends → p. 44

● *Organ recitals*
Classical music concerts like this can often cost a lot of money, but in many of Hamburg's churches you don't pay a thing, such as the *Stunde der Kirchenmusik* (hour of church music) that takes place every Wednesday in St Petri – for decades part of the Hamburg music repertoire → p. 34

● *Red bikes*
The environmentally-friendly way: the *Hamburger Stadträder* (city bikes) can be used by anyone and for the first 30 minutes are free – a great service for locals and tourists alike (photo) → p. 124

● *Water fountains and Maurice Ravel*
The free water-light concerts in the *Planten un Blomen* park take place every evening in the summer. There is an alternating programme, and the audience is always enthralled when the fountains, colours and music mix. A wonderful way to end the day → p. 38

●●●● Dots in the guidebook refer to 'Best of...' tips

### 🔵 On the Alster

A real Hamburger is one that goes for a sail at lunchtime. If you don't have your own boat, you can rent one from *Segelschule Pieper* or *Käpt'n Prüsse* and take to the waters of the Alster (photo) → p. 124

### 🔵 Fischmarkt (fish market)

You've passed the test when you skip the Sunday sleep-in and get up at dawn for a visit to the *Fischmarkt*. Here there are stalls selling fresh fish, seafood, fruit and foodie treats – great atmosphere! → p. 50

### 🔵 Water, stars and music

The *Elbphilharmonie* concert hall is the city's newest and already most popular landmark. Concert tickets are hard to get, but the 37 m/121.4 ft high plaza is open to the public. Why not visit in the evening? The ships' lights glimmer below, and you can see the moon's reflection on the wavy roof with its 1 100 curved windows → p. 43

### 🔵 Panorama with remoulade sauce

It's always really busy at the *shipping piers* in St Pauli. Get an extra-large fish roll, then climb the few steps to the observation deck and watch the action from above → p. 38

### 🔵 On water and land

How about a city bus tour? Or a harbour tour with a barge? That's nothing compared to Hamburg's *Hafencity Riverbus*. The bus rolls off the street onto water. But get ready for some screaming among the passengers when the bus floats onto the water! → p. 124

### 🔵 Wanderlust

Sleep with the mariners at the *Seemannsmission* – it's simple, cheap and right by the River Elbe. The night-time view of the water and old cranes makes you long for distant lands. As the song goes by Hans Albers: 'Seemannsbraut ist die See ...' ('A mariner's bride is the sea ...') → p. 97

### 🔵 On the Reeperbahn at 12.30am

No visit to Hamburg is complete without a walk along the *Reeperbahn*. If you find the red light district a little too scary on your own, you can book a *'Historical Whore Tour'*. Extremely insightful and not seedy → p. 40

ONLY IN

# BEST OF ...

● **Undercover**
*Rain?* In Hamburg you don't need to let a bit of rain get in the way of your shopping. For this is the city of *shopping arcades*. You can just about keep your feet dry all the way from the Jungfernstieg to Mönckebergstraße → p. 77

● **The thicker the better**
Whether the foghorns are sounding on the Elbe or there's a howling gale makes no odds to guests in the *Tower Bar* on the 12th floor of the *Hotel Hafen Hamburg* – they can simply relax and watch from above (photo) → p. 95

● **Stylish and dry**
At the *Stilwerk* on Große Elbstraße you can browse and buy beautiful furniture and home accessories, and at weekends there is even childcare → p. 75

● **Tunnel vision**
The steps lead steeply down, while cars shudder into the deep aboard the adjacent vehicle lift. The walk through the tiled tube of the *Alter Elbtunnel* is a very special experience. At the other end you take the lift up and look across at the city's church spires when you emerge → p. 36

● **The world in miniature**
*Miniatur-Wunderland* (miniature wonderland) in the Speicherstadt really lives up to its name. You could spend hours watching the trains, the traffic, and the aeroplanes taking off and the lights coming on, and marvel at the extraordinary attention to detail → p. 45

● **Quality time with art**
The entrance is via the new (actually historically correct) main entrance into the wonderfully refurbished Hamburger *Kunsthalle* with its redesigned exhibition spaces on Contemporary Art or the Old Masters → p. 33

**RAIN**

# RELAX AND CHILL OUT
## Take it easy and spoil yourself

● *All steamed up*
A good slap of lather on your back and strong hands massaging away all the tension. At the original *Turkish hamam*, you can forget all about your cares → **p. 35**

● *Where the willows weep*
Almost inaudibly, the white *Alster steamers* ply the canals around the Außenalster lake. The noise of the big city is far away – an ideal place to switch off (photo) → **p. 122**

● *Go with the flow ...*
Bathe in the heated water (32 °C/90 °F) where you can drift along WITHOUT the mobile phone ringing, but with underwater music – the *Kaifu-Sole* in Hamburg's oldest, beautifully renovated spa is unique → **p. 124**

● *Relaxing on the Elbe beach*
On the *Strandperle* at Övelgönne you can feel the sand between your toes, sip a drink and enjoy the view across the Elbe → **p. 51**

● *Room to breathe*
For free and gloriously peaceful: relax in the *Planten un Blomen* park, a city-centre oasis created on the site of the old ramparts. Lie by the lake or sit on the benches and huge wooden chairs amidst plants and flowers → **p. 56**

● *Stay afloat amidst industrial charm*
The Café *Entenwerder 1* is on a pontoon in dreamy Rothenburgsort. Guests sit on furniture made from old mooring posts; they sip aromatic coffee and admire the bridges and pontoons and look forward to the cycle ride back on Hamburg's most fantastic cycle path → **p. 18**

● *Wellness in the hotel*
Since the majority of hotel guests are usually out and about during the day, chances are the spa facilities in the better hotels are relatively empty and therefore wonderfully peaceful. In many establishments non-residents are also welcome, such as at the *Grand Elysée* at the Dammtor → **p. 92**

# INTRODUCTION

# DISCOVER HAMBURG!

Wind and water – these are the elements that define Hamburg. On a sunny day there's no nicer place to be than the shore of the Außenalster lake: swans and sailing boats and views of luxury villas across the water. While on a stormy day there's nowhere more exciting than the port and its shipping piers, the *Landungsbrücken*: *waves, tug boats and giant container ships*. No other city in Germany can boast such growth in its visitor numbers. The only question is: when are you going to come?

There are days on which even die-hard Hanseatics are surprised by their city. On a summer evening they sit with their beer on the beach by the Elbe at Övelgönne, with container ships, harbour ferries and sailing boats passing right in front of them. They take a stroll towards the city centre, past the modern developments of the Elbmeile, gaze across the water from the Dockland office block that juts out over the river and take a detour for a nightcap at the St Pauli *beach club*. The stroll continues to *Hafencity*, where there will probably be another festival going on – jazz or literature. They might hang around for a bit and admire the imposing tinted glass façade of the *Elbphilharmonie*, which towers over the river. Even now, late in the evening, visitors are still strolling on the square. Mobile phone cameras flash – the view is spectacular. In the background, the new developments of the Hafencity and the illuminated façades of the *Speicherstadt* (warehouse district) are visible. By this stage these Hamburgers will have looked at each other and said something like: wow, we really do live in a great city!

## It's boom time in the 'far north'

The Hanseatics are not alone in this observation. The tourist office recently recorded more than 12 million overnight stays per year, more than ever before. The population of Germany's second-largest city has also been growing for years, soon set to pass the 1.8 million mark. The 'far north' is regarded as the economic powerhouse for an entire region and has recovered from the economic crisis faster than expected. Unemployment is falling and all over the city there is building work going on and new schemes being planned. Hamburg has even become the *focus of international attention*, and at the start of 2017 'The New York Times' even ranked the city as one of the world's top tourist destinations. 'A heaven for architecture and design.' Wow! For many the transformation of the city's image has come as something of a surprise. It wasn't always thus: Hamburg used to be the city of *Pfeffersäcke* – or moneybags – who don't even know how to spell the word 'culture'; the city with the boring brick buildings, the city where it always seems to rain …

The new showstopper in Hafencity – the Elbphilharmonie

The turning point in the city's fortunes focuses on the period just before the fall of the Berlin Wall. Hamburg's mayor at the time was Henning Voscherau and on trips to East Germany he realised one thing: the Wall would ultimately fall. In a free Europe the city of Hamburg could develop into a *trading hub between east and west*, but for that to happen it first had to be 'woken up from its self-satisfied afternoon nap', as Voscherau put it. So planning went ahead for a fourth Elbtunnel, the expansion of the airport, the Airbus site; schemes for new container terminals such as at Altenwerder were forced through against opposition. And above all: in secret negotiations the city began buying up land in the harbour area; in secret mainly to avoid speculation. In May 1997, at the *Überseeclub* on the Alster, Voscherau presented his master plan for the port city to the crème de la crème of the Hanseatic business world: 'returning the inner city to the water can become a reality'. Now this reality has arrived and anyone with the means will buy a *loft at the Lohsepark* or move their solicitor's chambers to a warehouse on Alten Wandrahm in the Speicherstadt. The area has schools, several kindergartens, a

> **Things are happening here – and not just in Hafencity**

university and a science centre. *On warm summer evenings, the quays and cafés are a hive of activity* with many cultural events taking place. The headquarters of Greenpeace, with wind turbines and solar panels on the roof, is at the *Magdeburger Hafen*; the *Lohsepark* features a memorial to the Jews who were deported from Hamburg, and residential buildings on stilts are under construction in the water at the *Baakenhafen*. So everything is hunky-dory in the shiny, new Hafencity world? Not quite. Architects and city planners rail against (some say more or less 'puked up') boring buildings; transport links leave a lot to be desired; numerous promises have been made which have not been kept (e. g. a sports ground for the Hafencity Sports Club). Despite the massive hype surrounding Hamburg's new landmark, the Elbphilharmonie – nobody has quite forgotten the scandal about extortionate costs and endless building delays – as critics of this project frequently remind people.

Its official name is the Free and Hanseatic City of Hamburg. But more than the Hanseatic League, that great maritime trading block of the Middle Ages, it was their *freedom* that inhabitants always valued most, and that included freedom from kings, from chancellors and from prelates; freedom from federal-state mergers and prime ministers. The long debated merging of the north-German states will probably remain a vision. As well as attachment to hearth and home, there is *wanderlust*. The tooting of ships is still heard in the neighbourhoods where seagulls do not cry and floods do not break through the walls.

A prejudice is that Hamburgers are arrogant. But you wouldn't notice it as a tourist walking through the city. The Hamburgers are more helpful, more open and friendly than you would expect. Many speak excellent English – the relationship to the trading partner on the other side of the Channel has always been a strong one. And continuing in this vain, *the Hamburger is also liberal-minded*. Whether a life-long punk on Hafenstraße or slick sales promoter, everyone can be just as he or she is. But there is one thing required of everyone: attitude. Here the Hanseatic remains true to his or her mentality – never loses composure and always exercises restraint. Such expectations applied to politicians like Helmut Schmidt just as much as to actors, media people, and captains of industry and every normal citizen of the city. Being over-pretentious is frowned upon here. For true Hanseatics, actual profit is far more important than outward appearances. It is claimed that

> **Enterprising yet liberal-minded and cosmopolitan**

Hamburg is now home to more millionaires per capita than any other city in Europe. For many, it seems, *business acumen* is in their blood. Achieving your goal is not for the faint-hearted. One of the best examples of this is the way Hamburg went about celebrating its *annual anniversary as a port*. It was once thought that Emperor Frederick Barbarossa issued a charter for trade on the Elbe on 7 May 1189. In fact, this document was uncovered as a forgery as far back as 1907, but such a minor detail was never going to stop the Hamburgers celebrating their festival to mark the event – and making a tidy profit putting on the world's biggest port festival.

*People enjoy living here and they like to show it*. Hamburg is headquarters to over 1 300 charitable foundations – the Hanseatic city tops the league for Germany! And whether students or millionaires, all delegates to the Hamburg 'donation parliament' have a say in how their money is spent: on the Hamburg Ballet or the *Polittbüro* theatre and comedy club; on rock events at the *Uebel & Gefährlich* or on children's theatre. Culture has long been part of everyday life here, even if it slips every now and then. For example, many alternative artists have headed for Berlin where the climate is said to be much more supportive. Indeed high culture has always had it much easier in Hamburg than the experimental variety – for instance *the city has more than 60 theatres* – many of which get by with no support. Hamburg will not host the Olympic Games again soon – in a referendum held in autumn 2015 a narrow majority voted against participating in a new bid for the games.

# VERY BRITISH, INDEED!

Centuries of trading relations with Great Britain explain why many Hanseatics love to appear eccentric. Men wear blue blazers with club badges, while women sport brogues, pearl necklaces and pleated skirts. Milestone birthdays are celebrated at the *Anglo German Club*. At 6am they go rowing on the Alster or meet for 'high goal polo' in the small pool on the front lawn of the polo club. Sons and daughters of wealthy patrons attend summer college and play tennis or hockey in their leisure time. In 2006, there was the shock closure of the British consulate on the Alster. Ever since there has 'only' been an honorary consulate in Hamburg. And now Brexit – 'keep calm and carry on'!

But Hamburg's residents are not against sport. Joining in is more important than being a spectator. People love jogging, cycling, stamina sports – whether that's marathons or rowing, cycle races or skating. The most spectacular public event is the triathlon held in summer. Tourists can also register and can enjoy a contrasting view of the city skyline in the swimming competition on the Alster. One side effect of so many big events is that

**Ultra-sporty – even without the Olympics**

on fine summer weekends the downtown areas are often blocked off. That means endless traffic queues and jams! But native Hamburgers are familiar with this: there is always a new building site somewhere – e.g. for the next few years a major motorway extension over the A7 will extend the Elbtunnel. It's advisable to leave the car behind.

Adventure playground in the city centre: beach by the Elbe near Övelgönne

*Hamburg is one of the greenest cities in Germany* with a lake right in the middle. Water from below and from above – indeed the weather doesn't always play fair. But rain and fog don't bother the real Hanseatics because there's always compensation in those glorious days when there's a fresh breeze and the air is so clear that you really want to fill your lungs with it. So why should you visit Hamburg? Very simply, *because it is so beautiful here*. The Elbe and the Alster offer fantastic panoramic views, and you have a good overview of the city. Even if you just have a weekend it's easy to plan a tour with all the best highlights. If you have more time, go over to Veddel. There, at the historic shed number 50, is the Harbour Museum. At weekends volunteers work here on the old boats. They will tell you what seafaring used to be like. And then go to the end of the quay (the Hansahöft) and look across: over there, the wavy facade of the Elbphilharmonie glimmers in the sunlight. It is the past, present and future all in one place.

# WHAT'S HOT

## 1 Go slow

**Hamburg on boards** Standup paddleboarding is the new craze which offers competition in the summer for the yachts on the Außenalster lake. If you'd like to try it, these four skills are a must: climbing on the board, standing up, staying upright when paddling, plus looking good even as you fall into the water. You can hire paddle boards in several places on the Alster. Courses are available, for example, at the *SUP Club Hamburg (Noas Bootsverleih | Isekai 1 | supclubhamburg.de)*.

## Wild east

## 2

**Creative set** This is no place for luxury, but the creative set are thriving in Rothenburgsort. This district was neglected for a long time and is only 2 km/1.2 mi from the city centre. It offers a lake, green parks, the brick industry and plenty of active residents. 'Hamburg's wild east' *(hwo-digital.de)* was the initiative that first campaigned for a cycle route from the Deichtorhallen into the centre of this district, then two artisans restored the old petrol station *brandshof (tankstelle-brandshof.de)* (photo) and classic cars now queue up. An old customs pontoon houses ● Café *Entenwerder 1 (daily | Entenwerder 1)* which is hugely popular.

## 3 Kiez gourmets

**Meals on wheels** Rugged guys serve vegan food and homemade chips, a cheerful Parisian gives out funky hotdogs, two female chefs provide Polish piroshky – street food is a way of life. The food waggons are more like gourmet kitchens on wheels than snack bars. You can find them almost anywhere in Hamburg. A firm favourite for gourmets is the *St. Pauli Straßenmampf* at Spielbudenplatz *(Thu 5pm–10pm | spielbudenplatz.eu/en)* and the *Food Truck Market (Tasköprüstr. 10 | food-trucks-hamburg.de)* in Bahrenfeld *(Sun 1pm–6pm)*.

# We're the traffic!

*Riding high in the saddle* Tough racing cyclists, trendy e-bikers and mums with kids in trailers – on the last Friday of every month hundreds of Hamburg residents join in the *Critical Mass (https://criticalmass.hamburg/)*. 'We don't block the traffic, we are the traffic!' is the motto of Germany's biggest 'critical mass'. For several minutes, the group cycles over the Reeperbahn or Mönckebergstrasse, while car drivers (with no option) stand still and look amazed. Only every second household in Hamburg owns a car, while practical freight bikes are everywhere. The bike shop *Ahoi Velo (Kleiner Schäferkamp 12 | www.ahoi-velo.de)* in the Schanzenviertel also rents bikes. When the next *Critical Mass glides* past, it's clear that Hamburg is well on its way to becoming a biking city.

# Tasty

*Craft beers* They go by the name of 'Hopper Bräu', 'Kreativbrauerei' or 'von Freude' – Hamburg's numerous microbreweries are signalling nothing short of a beer revolution: get rid of that tasteless industrial swill! Put some flavour back into those glasses! Scene bars stage beer tastings, e. g. at the *Galopper des Jahres* pub in *Haus 73* (p. 83). Kiosks in the trendy districts and the *Craft Beer Store (Lagerstr. 30a | www.craftbeerstore.de)* in the Schanzenviertel stock bottles of the stuff. If you like things a little more refined, the *Altes Mädchen (Lagerstr. 28b | en.altes-maedchen.com)*, the pub at the Ratsherren Brewery, serves an amazing 60 (!) different craft beers from all over the world.

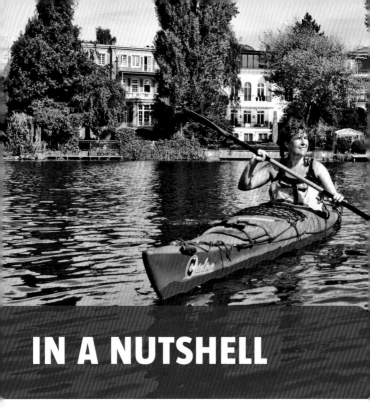

# IN A NUTSHELL

## GREEN CITY

Hamburg is green: there is the Elbe and the Alster, between them the major parks and green spaces and still relatively tolerable traffic that make life here so agreeable. While Hamburg was named 'Green Capital of Europe' for 2011, the far north still has some way to go in the environmental protection stakes. The city wanted a 40 per cent reduction in its $CO_2$ emissions by 2040 – now the goal is 'by 2050'. A coal-fired power station was built in Moorburg in 2015 – which isn't exactly progressive. For most Hamburgers, waste separation is still unheard of. The public transport system is well developed, but expensive, and people find it difficult to understand the complex fare structure of zones and rings. But there's one thing that has really been a resounding success: the funky red city bikes! This is hardly surprising as the first 30 minutes are free, and even non-sporty types are keen to have a ride. The question remains of the city authorities: why don't they apply the same principal to the public transport system? Buses and trains could be free for the first half hour. Surely this is a brilliant idea and something worthy of a Green Capital.

## AHOY!

If there's one thing that unites native Hamburgers then it's the 'waterfront' along the banks of the River Elbe and Alster. The slightest, most miserable waterside view (estate agents are famed for their advice, 'look as far as

Photo: In a kayak on the Außenalster

## Moneybags, ships and the Hanseatic people: characteristics and noteworthy features of Hamburg

you can out of the window and you'll glimpse the sails on the horizon') sends rents and square footage prices sky-rocketing. Hanseatic citizens also love plays on words: a Hamburg coffee roaster is known as 'Elb gold', day-care centres are 'Elb kids', the trendy drink is 'Ahoy fizz', the children's choir is the 'Alsterspatzen' and the daily news bulletin is called 'Elb impressions', while the new concert hall is abbreviated as 'Elphi'. Even funeral services adopt the phrase – for instance, the 'Alster Undertakers'. For

visitors, however, the main point is that it's impossible to visit Hamburg without a waterside excursion – whether it's on the Alster or the Elbe.

## ONCE IN THE HANSETIC LEAGUE, ALWAYS ...

HH – these are the first two letters on the number plates of all cars registered in Hamburg and they stand for 'Hansestadt Hamburg'. Between the 13th and 15th centuries Hamburg belonged to the Hanseatic League, at the time the most powerful city alliance in the world. There is little left now in the city to remind us of those days, unlike in Rostock, Bremen and Lübeck. If there is one legacy that has survived to the present it is the Hanseatic mentality. A Hanseatic merchant embodies many virtues: he is proud of his traditions, is honest and direct, but never short-tempered. A true Hanseatic citizen doesn't look back ('what's done is done ...'), but forward.

# FLOODING

First of all: had there been no flooding in 1962, Helmut Schmidt – who was Minister for Internal Affairs in Hamburg at the time – would not have been able to demonstrate that he had the makings of a future German Chancellor. When the banks burst in Wilhelmsburg, the decisive action he took saved the lives of thousands of people. The subject has now become more a myth than a fact: the plaques that commemorate the great floods in Övelgönne and in Blankenese tell of a certain pride – 'look at us now; we even survived that'. The subject is, however, deadly serious. Climate

experts in Hamburg reckon with a long-term rise in sea level of 30 cm/1 ft. The 103 km/64 mi long embankment in the city has been or is still in the process of being raised to a height of 9.25 m/30 ft. The planned dredging of the Elbe shipping lane has come in for a lot of criticism: as the river runs faster, the tide will come in faster and with greater force. New developments take account of the flooding threat: in Hafencity all new buildings are constructed on plinths and in emergencies residents can be evacuated via higher-lying streets or bridges. The neighbouring historic Speicherstadt (warehouse district) on the other hand is exposed to the smallest rise in sea levels – and you are not really supposed to live there. However, given a suitable escape route, it is possible – the first hotels have already arrived!

# HAMBURG – HIGH AND LOW

There is a fabulous view from here: Süllberg in Blankenese is 75 m/246.1 ft high. The terrace of the Energiebunker (former air-raid bunker) in Wilhelmsburg

# FIT IN THE CITY

Whichever route you take, you will never be alone on Hamburg's most popular running mile. Somebody is always running along the 7.4 km/4.6 mi circuit around the Außenalster – you can enjoy many wonderful impressions of Hamburg on the way. At night-time, Hamburg is a haven for tiderunners: *(facebook.com/tiderunnershh)*, a group that jogs across streets, squares, through underground tunnels or even a shopping centre. The runners travel 15 km/9.3 mi come rain

or shine – and no headphones! Starting time is Wed 9pm in front of the *Superbude in St Pauli* (see p. 98). Germany's best ice skating rink is located at the old ramparts between Neustadt and St Pauli: in winter, you can spin pirouettes in the open air. From April to October, skaters are allowed to use the area free of charge *(mid-Nov–mid-March daily 10am–10pm, Wed to 5pm | 5.50 euros for 2.5 hr | Holstenwall 10 | www.eisarena-hamburg.de | U 3 St Pauli)*.

Queen Mary 2 visits St Pauli: the luxury liner off the Landungsbrücken

is 30 m/98.4 ft high, the viewing platform of the 'Michel' stands 106 m/348 ft high (Michel Church tower, the main square at the Elbphilharmonie is raised 37 m/121.4 ft – and since we're talking about the 'Elphi': 40 m/131.2 ft underground is Hamburg's deepest U-Bahn line towards Elbbrücken. That's too deep to hop off – the next stop is at Überseequartier. At 19.5 m/64 ft below ground, it's still incredibly deep – by comparison: the U-Bahn at Jungfernstieg is just 6 m/19.7 ft below ground.

## MONEYBAGS

This derogatory term (in German *Pfeffersäcke*) for the enterprising merchants of Hamburg, likely used in connection with any conceivable subject in Hamburg, has a long tradition. It was first used by Denmark's King Christian IV (1577–1649). A quotation from one of his letters about the citizens of Ham-

burg says it all: 'Arrogant skinflints and moneybags, slimy fishmongers and lazybones ...'

## QUEEN MARY & CO

When the 'Queen Mary' comes to town, Hamburgers as well as tourists line the banks of the Elbe by the thousand. They wave and jostle around, there is special coverage of the event on television, bakers bake bread rolls in the shape of a ship: it's party time on the Elbe. The number of cruise ships arriving in Hamburg increases year on year. The *Cruise Days* have become a huge event. The biggest and most beautiful cruise ships visit Hamburg every September. At night, they cruise down the Elbe, bathed – like half the port and other parts of the city – in a mysterious blue light: The INSIDER TIP *Blue Port* is a creation of light artist and theatre maker Michael Batz. Meanwhile, there are various cruise terminals between Altona and Steinwerder, and building works are ongoing at Hafencity.

# BUSINESS CARDS

A strange heading, you might think. Who in the era of bluetooth still has a business card? Well, a lot of people in Hamburg. After all, it isn't just the name that's printed on the card, but it also tells people about where you come from in Hamburg, or how far you've come. And that is the all-important question: to the west or east of the Alster? New residents may think it doesn't matter whether you live in Eppendorf (to the west) or Winterhude (to the east): there are fabulously beautiful old houses in both districts, nightmarishly high rents, plenty of pubs, cafés and chic restaurants. For a true Hamburger, there's a world of difference between them (and not only the Alster). You don't have to understand – that's just the way it is.

# LEAP ACROSS THE ELBE

The Elbe belongs to Hamburg, like the Thames to London – no question. But somehow it does have a certain divisive nature. Harburg? Wilhelmsburg? Veddel? Generations of Hanseatic residents from the 'real' Eppendorf, Othmarschen or Volksdorf have never set foot there in their lives. A change is due – and is in fact under way. Hafencity has fundamentally changed the relationship of many Hamburgers to their city. The U-Bahn line 4 connects such exotic locations as Elbbrücken with the old familiar Jungfernstieg, and there are already a great number of cycle routes heading south. Across the Elbe in a word: for many Hamburgers the leap is just a short hop …

Representative, functional architecture: the Water Castle in the Speicherstadt

# THE CITY BELONGS TO US

For decades, nay centuries, urban planning in Hamburg followed the same pattern. Whether the Speicherstadt or a working-class district, an airport or port extension – wherever anything stood in the way of Hanseatic pursuit of profit it was relocated, torn down or built anew without anyone caring very much. But in recent years citizens have been getting increasingly vocal in their opposition to certain developments. You might have Gucci ladies from the Elbe suburbs planning sit-ins for the preservation of the Altona Museum, celebrities organising concerts in the Gängeviertel to prevent the eviction of the arts scene, and on the Reeperbahn furious citizens campaigned for a say in the rebuilding of the legendary 'Esso skyscrapers'. Hamburg's second major building project after Hafencity is 'Neue Mitte Altona'. On the old railway land between Altona and Diebsteich thousands of new apartments will be developed: there will also be plenty of housing set aside for alternative lifestyles – having a say is guaranteed! In the Schanzenviertel, where for years there has been a bitter struggle for the preservation of the *Rote Flora* community centre. At the same time, the latter district is experiencing a yuppie-style boom that no one had expected to happen so quickly. *www.recht aufstadt.net* is one of the websites that summarises the various campaigns taking place in the city.

# NOT WITHOUT MY BRICK

As Fritz Schumacher, the head of the city's planning department back in the mid 1920s once put it: 'brick makes constructing new buildings that much easier in the best possible way.' The director of the Art Gallery, Alfred Lichtwark, described his ideal building as follows: 'simple bricks with light mortar joints' with a 'roof of red tiles' and, please, 'no columns, ornament or timber framing'. Brick buildings are a feature of the city and can be found everywhere, from detached houses in Ohlsdorf to housing estates in Barmbek, from the old Speicherstadt warehouse district down by the harbour to Hafencity. Some years ago there was a fierce dispute between proponents of brick and those of glass. Architects such as Hadi Teherani were making the people of Hamburg furious with their new glass palaces. Modern is fine – but in brick please! That's how it was in the past and that's how it should stay. And by the way, the fascinating annual publication brought out by the local literature crowd is called 'The Hamburg Brick' – and there's nothing old-fashioned about that!

# SIGHTSEEING

**WHERE TO START?**
**Jungfernstieg** (133 D3)
(*L6*): Here you'll have a view over the Binnenalster lake, and there is one chic shop after another. To the left, on Neuer Jungfernstieg, you can see the facade of the noble Vier Jahreszeiten hotel. It's only a few steps through the Alster-Arkaden to the Rathausmarkt with the impressive *Rathaus* (city hall), from where the Mönckebergstraße shopping street leads to the main railway station. Several U- and S-Bahn lines stop at Jungfernstieg station, and there are buses at the Rathausmarkt and car parks in the area.

Hamburg city centre is compact: whether it's shopping, culture, the excitement of the port or catching your breath in a park – everything is within walking distance.

The most important message to all visitors to Hamburg is: leave the car behind. Apart from a few exceptions, Hamburg's attractions can all be reached by U- and S-Bahn or even by boat, and parking in the city is scarce (and expensive). The Hamburg Card *(www.hamburg-travel.com)* will provide you with free travel on public transport, or in good weather you can always take a red city bike (see p. 124) and cycle from one destination to the next.

Primarily, the many interesting museums in the centre will entice you to

## A green harbour metropolis on the rivers Elbe and Alster: cosmopolitan, sporting, culturally-engaged and business-minded

stop; all are located in close proximity to each other.

From the Rathaus to Hafencity it's almost half a mile as the crow flies. Between them, amongst other things, lies the old Speicherstadt warehouse district, which is Hamburg's jewel on the River Elbe. It became a Unesco World Heritage Site in 2016, which is entirely justified: the fantastic, closed ensemble of warehouses from the late 19th and early 20th centuries in the typical Hamburg red brick style is unique in the

world and thanks to a special lighting concept it also looks amazing at night.

If you have just a bit more time then you can experience Hamburg's great diversity: Eppendorf, St Georg, Altona, Winterhude, Eimsbüttel and Blankenese were all once villages or small towns independent of Hamburg. All of them have their nice little peculiarities that are worth discovering. And everywhere there are wonderful pubs, good restaurants, whimsical boutiques, colourful shops, markets, theatres and cinemas.

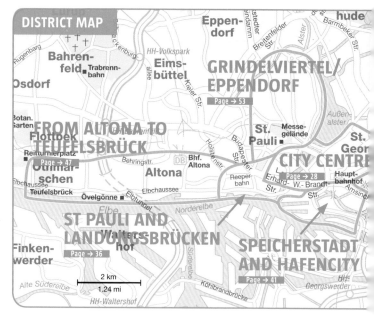

The map shows the location of the most interesting districts. There is a detailed map of each district on which each of the sights described is numbered.

# CITY CENTRE

**In the city centre it's mostly about one thing: spending money. There's one shopping arcade after another with everything ranging from luxury boutiques to department stores and expensive restaurants to simple snack bars.**

Amid all this commercialism you should not neglect the cultural side of things. Some of the best museums are situated right here in the heart of the city, and even if you don't have much time they're still worth a visit. And then of course there's the magnificent *Rathaus* (city hall), with the following inscription high above the doorway: *Libertatem quam peperere maiores digne studeat servare pos-*

*teritas*: 'May the freedoms won by their forebears be preserved with dignity by future generations'. A good motto to remember when strolling about town.

### ■ ALTSTADT
(132–133 C–E5) (*ⓜ L–M7*)

Hamburg's old town is built around the historic Elbe port on the Nikolaifleet canal. Almost nothing now remains of the original buildings. Almost all medieval structures fell victim to the fire of 1842, or were subsequently demolished. Great mercantile office blocks, the *Kontorhäuser*, were built in their place. But since the end of the war not as much has changed here as in other parts of Hamburg. Take a stroll along the Altstädterstraße or Burchardstraße. You will still find the cobbler who knows all his customers, a hat maker and one of the oldest tea shops in Germany, the *Teehandlung Ernst Zwack (Kattrepelbrücke 1)*. Along the Altstädter Twiete are the offices of Hamburg's newspaper for the homeless *Hinz & Kunzt. U 3 Mönckebergstraße*

## ▣ BINNENALSTER
### (133 D–E3) *(🕮 L–M6)*

The 'binnen' refers to the part of the lake that was 'inside' the city walls and is the very heart of the city. Take a seat at the Jungfernstieg quay and enjoy the view. Right in front of you is where the white Alster steamers cast off, with a few swans swimming around; in the middle of the Binnenalster is the impressive plume of the Alster Fountain – which at Christmas is replaced by a giant illuminated tree. The former millpond, which took on its present form after the Great Fire of 1842, covers an area of around 45 acres. During World War II it was covered over with cardboard dummies to fool enemy bombers. The technically complicated construction of the public transportation system began in 1967 and took over 15 years to complete. Today several underground and suburban railway lines run right underneath the Binnenalster. The most recent line is the U 4 to Hafencity. On your journey there you pass under the new Elbphilharmonie – there were insufficient funds for an U-Bahn station there (according to many experts the only sensible solution for the huge concert hall) … The website *u4.hochbahn.de* has lots of information. *S-/U-Bahn Jungfernstieg*

## ▣ BUCERIUS KUNST FORUM
### (133 D4) *(🕮 L6)*

Where would Hamburg be without its generous patrons? Gerd Bucerius, founder of the weekly newspaper 'Die Zeit', was one of them. In 2002, the Zeit Foundation, which he financed, established an exhibition centre in the former *Reichsbank* on Rathausmarkt. The curators have a knack for hosting sophis-

---

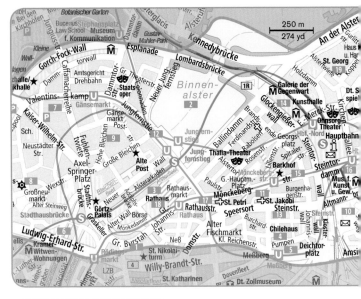

## SIGHTSEEING IN THE CITY CENTRE

ticated exhibitions that also appeal to a broader public. *Daily 11am–7pm, Thu until 9pm | admission 8 euros | Rathausmarkt 2 | tel. 040 3609960 | bucerius kunstforum.de/en | U 3 Rathaus*

### 4 CHILEHAUS (133 E5) (*M7*)

On its completion in 1924, the Chilehaus was regarded as one of the 'architectural wonders of the world'. If you stand at the corner beneath the sculpture of the eagle you can easily understand its fascination. Commissioned by the merchant Henry B. Sloman, the architect Fritz Höger used more than 4 million red bricks for its construction. Sloman made his fortune importing saltpetre from Chile, hence the name Chilehaus. You can see that in the charming animal figures with South American motifs (e.g. in the courtyard portal A, stairwell left). The building was considered a symbol of Hamburg's resurgence after World War I. *Stairwells open only during office hours | U 1 Meßberg*

### 5 CHOCOVERSUM (133 E5) (*M7*)

Okay, the main purpose behind this attraction might be to sell Hachez chocolate. But what the makers have created around the theme of 'how is chocolate made' is both informative and charming and therefore highly recommended. Warning for those with a sweet tooth: the chocolate is still warm from the mixer – simply delicious. *Daily 10am–6pm, guided tours only (90 min), last tour around 4.30pm | admission 15 euros | Meßberg 1 | tel. 040 41912300 | www.chocoversum.de/en | U 1 Meßberg*

### 6 FLEETINSEL (132 C4) (𝄞 L7)

A piece of old Hamburg has been preserved along Admiralitätsstraße and its adjacent *Fleeten* (canals). Today it is particularly popular with art lovers: some of the best galleries in the city are located in the old merchant houses here, renovated by a generous patron. You will also find the wonderful art bookshop of *Sautter + Lackmann. S 1, 3 Stadthausbrücke*

### 7 GÄNGEVIERTEL (132 B–C3) (𝄞 L6)

Artists and creative types stopped demolition plans. Now, the old buildings in the centre of Hamburg almost look establisheed and several are already listed buildings. But hopefully the heart of the Gängeviertel remains as rebellious as it ever was. 'We're a large and daily growing number' is the slogan of the cooperative that now looks after building conservation. It's worth paying a visit and taking part if you can. There are studios, readings, concerts and much more besides. *Valentinskamp/Caffamacherreihe | dasgaengeviertel.info/en | U2 Gänsemarkt*

### 8 GROSSNEUMARKT (132 B4) (𝄞 L7)

The 'big new market' (it acquired this name because there was already a smaller 'new market' near the Nicolaikirche) was once the assembly point for Hamburg's militia. Today there are lots of nice pubs on the Großneumarkt; in summer you can eat outside beneath roman-

tic lights. Take a short walk away from the square through the Neustadt – in contrast to the historic old city, this district used to lie outside the city walls. The new, expanding 'KomponistenQuartier', comprising prettily renovated, half-timbered houses in Peterstraße, has turned out particularly well. Small museums have been established to honour composers such as Johannes Brahms, Carl Philipp Emanuel Bach, Georg Philipp Telemann, among others. Kent Nagano, General Music Director of the Staatsoper Hamburg, is the project's patron. Information on the various sites and opening times at *www.komponistenquartier.de/short-english-version | S 1, 3 Stadthausbrücke*

Expressionist architecture: Chilehaus

**9 HANSEVIERTEL (132 C3) (∅ L6)**
Built in 1980, the Hanseviertel was the city's first large shopping centre. The Hamburg architect's firm of van Gerkan, Marg & Partners made their breakthrough with what was at the time a spectacular glass dome building. The champagne and lobster stand is a legend – for a luxury snack on a Saturday morning. *S-/U-Bahn Jungfernstieg*

**10 HÜHNERPOSTEN (133 F4) (∅ M7)**
A nice spot to warm up, surf the internet or read the newspaper, for this is the location of the *Zentralbibliothek*

storm in the last war – unlike the rest of the church that is obvious from the strikingly 'modern' church tower. Every Thu around noon there is a free guided tour and information about the baroque jewel and its 60 (!) stops. *Mon–Sat 10am–5pm, Oct–March 11am–5pm, tower open at irregular times | Jakobikirchhof 22 | www.jacobus.de/neu/english/index.html | U 3 Mönckebergstraße*

**12 JUNGFERNSTIEG (133 D3) (∅ L6)**
The Hamburgers call this 'the most beautiful shopping street in the world'. That might be a bit of an exaggera-

Young visitors to the old masters: kids in the Kunsthalle

*(central library: Mon–Sat 11am–7pm | Hühnerposten 1 | tel. 040 42 60 60 | www.buecherhallen.de | S-/U-Bahn Hauptbahnhof).* The two bronze figures on the forecourt were created by sculptor Stephan Balkenhol.

**11 JAKOBIKIRCHE (133 E4) (∅ M7)**
Organ fans listen up! Here, a precious Arp-Schnitger organ survived the fire-

tion, but in summer when you can eat ice cream and count the ships on the steps leading to the Alster, it's paradise here. Unfortunately commerce has completely taken over: in summer there's a never-ending series of street fairs with stalls. What would the writer Heinrich Heine have made of these colourful goings on? He really enjoyed poking fun at the Hanseatic 'moneybags' (merchants) while drinking his coffee in the Alster-pavillon. The 🔅 Alsterpavillon (now containing the *Alex café*) is still there today, however not so much a meeting place for intellectuals as for tourists and visitors from the suburbs. Be that as it may, the view from the terrace is still stunning. *S-/U-Bahn Jungfernstieg*

## 🔟 KONTORHAUSVIERTEL
(133 E4–5) (*∭ M7*)

The Kontorhausviertel was created between the late 19th century and early 20th century. It is the location of such enormous buildings as the *Chilehaus* or the *Sprinkenhof (Burchardstr. 4–6)*. On its completion in 1932 the latter was considered the largest office building in the world. The architects were Fritz Höger and the brothers Hans and Oskar Gerson. Note the net-like pattern on the façade and the gilded terracotta stones; the round stairwell is a masterpiece. The first *Kontorhaus* in Hamburg was actually the old *Dovenhof* on Brandstwiete. It was built by Martin Haller who was already a famous architect in his own lifetime. The Laeiszhalle, the Hapag Building on Ballindamm and the Rathaus are all by him. The Dovenhof was very modern in its day: there was a paternoster lift, an in-house postal service and the heating costs were charged precisely according to square metreage of space. Unfortunately, the badly damaged building was demolished at the end of the war. *U 1 Steinstraße, Meßberg*

## 🔟 KUNSTHALLE ★ ●
(133 E3) (*∭ M6*)

Hamburgers have an ambivalent relationship to their art. On the one hand they consider culture to be of 'prime importance' to the state, but on the other many don't seem to realise that their Kunsthalle is one of the most impor-tant art museums in Germany. The gallery is now even more attractive, thanks to substantial renovation work in recent years worth over 20 million euros, made possible by a generous donation by patrons Dorit and Alexander Otto. Go and see the old masters – in particular Master Bertram's altarpiece, and marvel at the masterpieces of classical modernism by artists ranging from Max Liebermann to Emil Nolde and Pablo Picasso. In the *Galerie der Gegenwart* – a cuboid building designed by Oswald Mathias Ungers and connected to the Kunsthalle via an underground passageway – you will find works by Gerhard Richter, Jeff Koons and Georg Baselitz. You can treat yourself to a break in the *Café Liebermann. Tue–Sun 10am–6pm, Thu until 9pm | admission 8 euros | Glockengießerwall 5 | www.hamburger-kunsthalle.de/en | S-/U-Bahn Hauptbahnhof*

## 🔟 MÖNCKEBERGSTRASSE
(133 D–E4) (*∭ M6–7*)

The elegant curve of this 29-m/95.1-ft-wide street was cut through the old city between 1908 and 1911. At the same time, the tunnel was dug for the underground. Craftsmen, coachmen and workers were moved out. *Kontorhäuser,* grand office buildings, were constructed and at the top end of Spitaler-straße, Fritz Schumacher designed the Mönckeberg Fountain to 'promote city living'. Today Mönckebergstraße is always busy, not to say packed. Previously, it was characterised mainly by cheap shops and sausage stands. The creation of the *Europa-Passage* brought an upswing. Also, drop by the *Kulturcafé* at the Mönckeberg Fountain. On the outside it's just a Starbucks; inside, however, it has information about and tickets for the Elbphilharmonie *(www.elbphilharmonie.de/en/how-to-book). U 3 Mönckebergstraße*

Where local policy is decided: chamber of the Hamburg Parliament in the Rathaus

### 16 MUSEUM FÜR KUNST UND GEWERBE (133 F4) (*M N6*)

The impressive building near the railway station has been undergoing renovations for years – now, everything has been completed, even the old gymnasium (formerly a school site) has been sympathetically restored and is used as an exhibition space. The legendary original canteen of weekly magazine 'Der Spiegel' is well worth a look. One can only admire the vision of the first museum director, Justus Brinckmann: in 1900 he purchased a complete art nouveau room in Paris. The museum is also renowned for its East Asia section; the authentic Japanese tea ceremony held in the Japanese teahouse is an institution (check the website for events). Break off for refreshments at the attractive museum café, *Destille. Tue–Sun 10am–6pm, Wed/Thu until 9pm | admission 12 euros | Steintorplatz | www.mkg-hamburg.de/en | S-/U-Bahn Hauptbahnhof*

### 17 PETRIKIRCHE (133 D4) (*M M7*)

With no regard for the injured pride of the residents of Hamburg, Napoleon's soldiers stabled their horses in this brick church, Hamburg's oldest parish church dating from 1195. And, as if that were not enough, shortly before Christmas 1813, the French commander ordered the citizens to stock up on provisions for the coming months. Those who could not do so were threatened with expulsion. Thousands spent a night full of fear and cold in the Petrikirche before being driven out of the city through the Millerntor gate on 25 December. A painting in the church now commemorates the event. Every Wednesday at 5.15pm you can listen to organ music during the popular ● *Stunde der Kirchenmusik (hour of church music; free admission). Mon–Fri 10am–6.30pm, Sat 10am–5pm, Sun 9am–8pm | Mönckebergstr. | www.sankt-petri.de | U 3 Rathaus*

### 18 RATHAUS ★ (133 D4) (*M M6*)

It's well worth taking a tour of the town hall: there's gold and splendour wherever you look, such as in the large Emperor's Hall, so called because it was here, on 19 June 1895, that Kaiser Wilhelm II celebrated the opening of the Kiel Canal. The great and the good of Hamburg still gather here every February, as they have done ever since 1356 to celebrate the Matthias feast along with 'representatives of those powers friendly towards Hamburg'. During the Great Fire of 1842, the old town hall near the Trost Bridge was blown up in the hope that this would help contain the blaze and prevent things getting worse. Subsequently there were decades of squabbles about a replacement building. It was not until 1880, when the architect Martin Haller established the 'Town Hall Builders' Society', that there was a breakthrough. The construction presented a big technical challenge. It was necessary to drive 4 000 pylons into the muddy, marshy ground near the Alster. Today, they still support the 111 m/364 ft wide and 70 m/229.7 ft long construction with its 112 m/367 ft high central tower. Luckily, the Rathaus suffered only slight damage in World War II and today it is regarded as one of Germany's most important historicist-style buildings. If your German's up to it, there are even INSIDER TIP guided tours in Plattdeutsch dialect! The restaurant in the rooms of the former town hall cellar is called *Parlament. Daily Mon–Fri 7am–*

*7pm, often also until 9pm, Sat 10am–6pm, Sun 10am–5pm | guided tours (approx. 45 min) Mon–Fri 10am–3pm, Sat 10am–5pm, Sun 10am–4pm, except when council in session | tickets 4 euros | Rathausmarkt 1 | tel. 040 4 28 31 20 64 | www.hamburg.com | U 3 Rathaus*

### 19 ST GEORG (145 E4) (∅ N6)

Trendy and colourful: St Georg is home for everyone including the LGBT community. Hamburg's Catholic cathedral is near the biggest Mosque; people of all colours and nationalities live here, alongside prostitution and hip hostels, multi-generation houses and student lodgings. Hans Albers grew up at Lange Reihe and there are plenty of organic stores and bookshops, trendy bars and shisha bars, a burger bar in an old sports hall and probably the coolest delicatessan in Hamburg. Amongst the shelves of beverages and (award-winning!) cheese counter there are occasional festive tables for wine-tastings *(Lange Reihe 110 | niemerszein.de)*. Cultural events are catered for: the *Kunsthalle* (see p. 33) and *Literaturhaus* (see p. 111) are on the edge of the district, while right at the heart is the *Kunstforum*

# TIME TO CHILL

Suffering from a hangover? Is the weather getting to you? Then head off to ● *Hamam Hafen Hamburg* **(132 A5) (∅ K7)** *(Mon–Sat 10am–10pm, Sun until 9pm | book in advance | from 30 euros | Seewartenstr. 10 | tel. 040 3 11 08 39 90 | www.hamam-hamburg.de | S-/U-Bahn Landungsbrücken)*. Located in a former port hospital you can start by sweating it out on one of

the marble benches before having a massage and finishing – wrapped up in towels and wearing a bathrobe – by drinking tea reclined on the comfortable cushions in the relaxation room. There are masseuses for the female guests. If this one is too busy for you, ask about the smaller one in the Karoviertel, the city's first hamam: cosier and very beautiful.

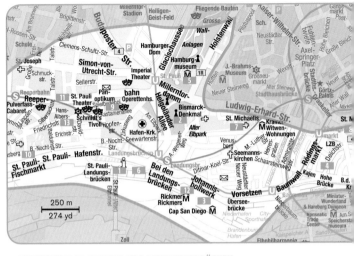

## SIGHTSEEING IN ST PAULI AND LANDUNGSBRÜCKEN

1. Alter Elbtunnel
2. Bismarck-Denkmal
3. Cap San Diego
4. Deichstraße
5. Hamburgmuseum
6. Landungsbrücken
7. Michaeliskirche
8. Nikolaikirchturm
9. Panoptikum
10. Park Fiction
11. Reeperbahn
12. Rickmer Rickmers
13. St Pauli Museum

*der GEDOK (Koppel 66 | www.gedok-hamburg.de), and the women artists' club founded in 1926 by artist Ida Dehmel: art by women, not only for women! S-/U-Bahn Hauptbahnhof*

# ST PAULI AND LANDUNGS-BRÜCKEN

**It's at the Landungsbrücken piers that the heart of Hamburg's harbour beats. Enjoy the hustle and bustle on the water. Take a walk through the Alter Elbtunnel and enjoy the view back over the city's skyline from Steinwerder. Sensational!**

A harbour cruise is a must for everyone – as is a visit to the Hamburg Museum and, of course, you simply have to climb Hamburg's landmark, the tower of the Michaeliskirche (St Michael's Church) where you might even hear the lone trumpeter playing a hymn tune. And then it's off to the Reeperbahn in the evening.

### 1 ALTER ELBTUNNEL ●
(144 A–B5) (ᗰ K7)

It rattles and shakes and is a real adventure: a descent with the car lift down (24 m/78.7 ft) to below the level of the Elbe. When the Alter Elbtunnel was built in 1911, it was an international sensation. It is 426.5 m/1399 ft long and originally served the harbour workers on their way to work. The dome on the shipping piers was modelled on the Pantheon in Rome. The tunnel is closed to cars at weekends. *Pedestrians and cyclists round the clock and free, cars only Mon–Fri 5.30am–8pm; never-ending renovation work means access to both tunnels is regularly disrupted | 2 euros | S-/U-Bahn Landungsbrücken*

## ▨ BISMARCK-DENKMAL ☼ (144 B5) (∅ K7)

This is the largest memorial in Hamburg; the figure alone is 15 m/49.2 ft high. It was unveiled in 1906 but was never popular and Rolf Liebermann, the former opera director, thought it 'an unparalleled monstrosity'. Even today, you won't find many residents of Hamburg here, in spite of the magnificent view of the harbour. The statue of Kaiser Wilhem I experienced a similar fate to that of the derided figure of the chancellor. The equestrian statue dating from 1889 was actually

planned for the Rathausmarkt but in 1930 it was moved to where it stands today, on the ramparts, just as resolutely ignored as good old Bismarck. *S-/U-Bahn Landungsbrücken*

## ▨ CAP SAN DIEGO (144 B6) (∅ L7)

This white, streamlined cargo vessel is moored at the Überseebrücke, where the cruise ships once berthed. Launched in 1961 as the last of a series of six ships, 'Cap San Diego' is the world's largest seaworthy civilian museum ship. Visitors can access virtually all areas of the vessel and it's even possible to take a cabin for the night *(80–120 euros). Daily 10am–6pm | admission 7 euros | Überseebrücke | tel. 040 36 42 09 | www.capsandiego. de | S-/U-Bahn Landungsbrücken*

## ▨ DEICHSTRASSE (134 C5) (∅ L7)

'Fire! Fire on Diekstraat!' This was the cry of the night watchman at one o'clock in

The Alter Elbtunnel, a listed monument that still fulfils its purpose

the morning of 5 May 1842. What happened over the next three days had a greater impact on Hamburg's appearance than all the destruction of World War II. The Great Fire reduced historic Hamburg to rubble. Under Alexis de Chateauneuf a new city was created: the 'Venice of the North' with the Alster-Arkaden and the Rathausmarkt. Today Deichstraße looks (almost) like it did in 1842. You can walk along the narrow passageways down to the canals and have a meal there on the jetty. At low tide this is not quite so pleasant – the sludge stinks! *U 3 Rödingsmarkt*

## ⑤ HAMBURGMUSEUM
**(132 A4)** *(𝄞 K6)*

The façade itself is pure splendour, and the interior of the museum on the site of the old city fortifications, which was planned by Fritz Schumacher and inaugurated in 1922, impresses with its magnificent staircases and halls. Let yourself be transported back to medieval times or to the Great Fire of 1842. From the bridge of the steamship 'Werner' you can observe Hamburg's harbour the way it was in 1938; you can track down the 'moneybags' in their original offices; or guide a model ship up through a lock. In a nutshell: here you can find everything relating to the history of Hamburg. There is even a miniature railway (switched on four times daily). If you grow tired visit the *Café Fees. Tue–Sat 10am–5pm, Sun 10am–6pm | admission 9 euros | Holstenwall 24 | tel. 040 428 13 21 00 | www.hamburgmuseum.de/en | U 3 St Pauli*

## ⑥ LANDUNGSBRÜCKEN ★
**(144 A–B 5–6)** *(𝄞 K7)*

If statistics are to be believed, the St.-Pauli-Landungsbrücken piers are – after the Brandenburg Gate in Berlin – Germany's second most visited tourist attraction. The pontoon installation was constructed between 1904–1910 and indeed, there is always nonstop bustle on the water with the continuous coming-and-going of the harbour ferries, interspersed by the catamaran to Helgoland or one of the two paddle steamers. The bridges are numbered to help with orientation. For example, the Hadag line ferry 62 is stationed at pier 3. Don't be put off by the commotion made by captains promoting their harbour tours, the harried commuters and day-trippers with their bikes. ● Buy a fish sandwich, find a place on the steps and watch the action from above. The promenade towards the city centre is new (and better protected against flooding). Stroll along here past the museum ships 'Cap San Diego' and 'Rickmer Rickmers' as far as the Hafencity. *S-/U-Bahn Landungsbrücken*

## 7 MICHAELISKIRCHE ★
(132 B4–5) (*L7*)

The Michaeliskirche (St Michael's Church) – is one of the city's most important landmarks. No other church is held in such esteem by the people of Hamburg. If the church needs attention, they rally and make donations. The present magnificent baroque building was designed by the architects Johann Leonard Prey and Ernst Georg Sonnin and was completed in 1786. After a fire completely destroyed the church in July 1906, the Senate immediately decided to reconstruct it on the same site, using the original plans. You should not leave Hamburg without visiting 'Michel'. Wonderful concerts are held here, for example during the Bach Weeks every autumn, and the Christmas concerts and services are very atmospheric when the white wood of the balustrades with its gold ornamentation is illuminated only by candlelight. The ⚘ tower is 132 m/433 ft high, and 452 steps lead to the top (there is also a lift). A tip is the INSIDER TIP *Nachtmichel (night Michel; start your climb to the right of the main entrance | in summer from around 7.30pm, in winter from 5.30pm | admission approx. 15 euros | tel. 0174 80 51 20 2 | nachtmichel.de):* at the top there is a small, heated room in the tower and something to drink – as well as the fantastic night-time view! You can also visit the crypt, which was only opened a few years ago. Hamburg's former musical director Philipp Emanuel Bach (1714–88) lies buried here. The second son of Johann Sebastian Bach succeeded Georg Philipp Telemann in the post in 1767.

Hamburg mix: 'Michel' & office blocks

*Daily May–Oct 9am–7.30pm, Nov–April 10am–5pm, (last admission in each case; visits are not possible during services), tower chorale Mon–Sat 10am and 9pm, Sun noon | church: free admission, crypt (with film) 4 euros, tower: 5 euros, combined ticket 7 euros | Englische Planke 1 | tel. 040 37 67 80 | www.st-michaelis.de | express bus 37 Michaeliskirche*

## 8 NIKOLAIKIRCHTURM ⚘
(133 D5) (*L7*)

The 147-m/482-ft tower was the only section of the Church of St Nicholas to survive the bombings of World War II, and it is now a memorial. The former main church was not very old at the time of its destruction, having been rebuilt in the style of a medieval Gothic cathedral after the Great Fire. The plans for that were drawn up by Gottfried Semper, the famous builder of the Semperoper in Dresden who came from Hamburg and earned his first laurels as a member of the 'Technical Commission'. Included in the admission fee of 5 euros for the war documentation centre is the ticket for the glass lift up the tower. At a height of 76 m/249.3 ft the viewing platform provides a fantastic panoramic view, which can be compared to the **INSIDERTIP** poignant photographs of the destroyed city. *May–Sept daily 10am–6pm, Oct–April until 5pm | english.mahnmal-st-nikolai.de | U 3 Rödingsmarkt*

### 9 PANOPTIKUM (144 A5) (*K7*)

Things are continually changing along the Reeperbahn – but the Panoptikum is still there, in the same spot it has occupied since 1879 and is now in the fourth generation and run by the great-grandson of the founder. 120 wax figures await you, including Harry Potter alias Daniel Radcliffe, style guru Karl Lagerfeld and Albert Einstein. *Mon–Fri 11am–9pm, Sat 11am–midnight, Sun 10am–9pm, closed Jan | admission 6 euros | Spielbudenplatz 3 | tel. 040 310317 | www.panoptikum.de/en | S 1, 3 Reeperbahn*

### 10 INSIDERTIP PARK FICTION (144 A5) (*J7*)

It is an exciting place, this rather offbeat little park at the edge of St Pauli, which enjoys a fantastic view of the harbour. It was born out of a local neighbourhood action group that managed to prevail against the developers. Now, you can sip a beer or latte under artificial palm trees among punks, market researchers and children playing ball. Right next door is the once embattled port road, below at the Fischmarkt, Hamburg's cult nightclub *Golden Pudel,* and right opposite, the floating docks of Blohm + Voss. All of which gives the area a really special atmosphere. *Corner Antonistr./Pinnasberg | park-fiction.net | S 1, 3 Reeperbahn*

### 11 REEPERBAHN ● (144 A–B5) (*J–K7*)

Come on, admit it: you are interested in the Reeperbahn. Where else can you so openly come into contact with a red-light district? Sex for money still plays a role, there are several thousand registered prostitutes and a large number who are not. During the day, the area is quite dreary but it becomes more co-

Summer vibe on the Reeperbahn: Spielbudenplatz by the 'Tanzende Türme' ('dancing towers')

lourful at night with the lights and neon signs. There are plenty of tours of the district, and many are loud and no longer an insider tip. The original version of these tours is more discreet, but no less intriuging: the **INSIDER TIP** *'Historical Whore Tour' (Thu–Sat 8pm, advance booking required, German speakers only | minimum age 18 | meeting point Davidwache | 29.50 euros | tel. 041 63 86 80 30 | www.hurentour.de)* But the district is changing. At the once legendary address of Reeperbahn Nr. 1 there now stand the *Tanzende Türme* (dancing towers) made of steel and glass, including ultra-chic restaurant *Clouds (www.clouds-hamburg. de | Expensive)* up on high, and the *Mojo Club* (p. 84) right at the bottom. New buildings are going up and relentless gentrification continues all around. But that doesn't mean that the whole 'Kiez' is suitable for all ages. Around Davidstraße, Talstraße or Hamburger Berg, prostitution, drugs and also criminal activity are common. The best way to get to know what's left of the street's glamorous side is the Reeperbahnfestival in autumn (p. 119): buy a ticket for all the clubs and dance through till dawn! *S 1, 3 Reeperbahn*

## 🔲 RICKMER RICKMERS
(132 A6) (*ⅅ K7*)

You can get a vivid idea of how hard a sailor's life was on Hamburg's first museum ship. It's pretty claustrophobic in a sailor's bunk, and the cook had to be something of an acrobat in the galley. Since 1987, the sleek, green sailing schooner has been moored in the Landungsbrücken at pier 1. Mail a postcard from here; the ship is after all an **INSIDER TIP** official marine post office. *Daily 10am–6pm | admission 5 euros | Landungsbrücken 1 | tel. 040 3 19 59 59 | www.rickmer-rickmers.de | S-/U-Bahn Landungsbrücken*

## 🔲 ST PAULI MUSEUM
(144 A5) (*ⅅ K7*)

The St Pauli veteran and photographer Günter Zint campaigned for years if not decades for a St Pauli Museum. In 2010 his dream finally came true. Of course not everything on display in the well-designed rooms is suitable for youngsters. Also part of the collection is the legacy of neighbourhood painter Erwin Ross. Conclusion when leaving: those were the days! *Tue–Sun from 11am until at least 9pm, Thu–Sun also longer | admission 5 euros | Davidstr. 17 | www.sankt-pauli-museum.de | S 1, 3 Reeperbahn*

# SPEICHER-STADT AND HAFENCITY

**The way the people of Hamburg have produced an entire district from scratch – wrested it from the Elbe – is astonishing. Only a few years ago, this was the site of the free port; sheds and cranes stood where the tenants of this area now look down on the Elbe from their loft apartments.**

There were similarly radical developments here once before: in order to make way for the warehouses of the ★ *Speicherstadt* (warehouse district) at the end of the 19th century, thousands of people were forced to leave their homes. Today the amazing ensemble of brick buildings is the jewel of the Hanseatic city. A worthwhile tip is to explore on foot and take a look at the inner courtyards at Holländische Brook and Alte Wandrahm. The warehouses look fantastic in the evenings in particular, thanks to a special lighting concept from Hamburg light artist Michael Batz. You can also explore Hafencity on foot. Get off at the Baumwall U-Bahn station (U3). From there it's just a few minutes to the Elbphilharmonie, the Kaiserkai and Lohsepark. Take a stroll along the quaysides and ask yourself the question: would you like to live here? A few thousand Hamburgers have already said yes. There's a school, a university, new U-Bahn stations, kindergartens and recreation grounds and, of course, many shops and, in the Überseequartier ('overseas quarter'), a Christmas market in December. Around Lohsepark and the Baakenhafen in the eastern part of Hafencity, large, new residential areas are being built. An exciting arts centre is planned for the ☀ Strandkai, to the right of the Unileverhaus and the Marco Polo Tower (an obscenely ugly, overpriced, concrete block of flats). There's a great view from here across the Elbe! Of course, things do go awry. Much of the architecture is on a vast scale and many buildings look the same with their boring and uniform design: like cubes, or boxes with glass – one much resembles the next. There's a lack of parking spaces and cycle routes, and the constant wind blow-

ing down the bare urban canyons can really get on your nerves. But in spite of all the moaning, no visit to Hamburg is complete without a look at Hafencity. *U 4 Überseequartier, Hafencity-Universität*

## ■1 DEICHTORHALLEN
(133 F5) (*M M7*)

This is where the market women from the surrounding area used to sell their wares, keeping their vegetables fresh in underground cellars. The Südhalle (south hall) is now the *Haus der Photographie* and often mounts exhibitions from the collection of F. C. Gundlach. Opposite, in the Nordhalle (north hall), are displays of contemporary art. The halls are just a 10-minute walk from the Hauptbahnhof and on the way you'll pass some galleries, the Kunstverein (art society) and the Academy of Arts, everything looking a bit inhospitable amid the roaring traffic, but often well worth closer inspection. The restaurant for the Deichtorhallen, *Fillet of Soul (daily | tel. 040 70 70 58 00 | Moderate),* is regarded as one of the city's trendy meeting places. *Tue–Sun 11am–6pm | admission 10 euros | Deichtor-*

Once fruit and veg, now art and photography: the Deichtorhallen

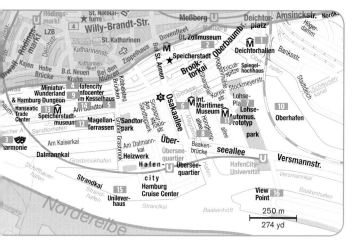

## SIGHTSEEING IN SPEICHERSTADT AND HAFENCITY

| | | |
|---|---|---|
| **1** Deichtorhallen | **6** Int. Maritimes Museum | **12** Sandtorhafen |
| **2** Dialoghaus in the Speicherstadt | **7** Lohsepark | **13** Speicherstadtmuseum |
| **3** Elbphilharmonie | **8** Magdeburger Hafen | **14** Spicy's |
| **4** Hamburg Dungeon | **9** Miniatur-Wunderland | **15** Unileverhaus |
| **5** Infocenter Kesselhaus | **10** Oberhafenquartier | **16** View point Hafencity |
| | **11** Prototyp | |

*str. 1–2 | www.deichtorhallen.de/en |
U 1 Steinstraße*

**2 DIALOGHAUS IN THE SPEICHER-
STADT (133 E5) (∅ M7)**
What is it like to be blind, to see nothing? Or to hear nothing? In this great museum (Dialogue in the Dark/Dialogue in Silence) you can experience what people with visual or hearing impairments live with all their lives. If you're not alone (one person can always be accommodated) you should definitely sign up in advance for a 60 or 90-minute tour. *Tue–Thu 9am–5pm, Fri 9am–7pm, Sat 10am–8pm, Sun 10am–6pm | Tickets 17 or 21 euros | Alter Wandrahm 4 | tel. 040 3 09 63 40 | www.dialog-in-hamburg.de/en | U 1 Meßberg*

**3 ELBPHILHARMONIE ★ ●**
**(132 C6) (∅ L7)**
The most important thing about the Elbphilharmonie is that you have to visit! Take a look for yourself! The ☀ plaza is open to visitors, but at peak times (especially weekends and public holidays) it's worth booking a timed ticket in advance (2 euros, online booking is best). Then, you can take the 82-m/269-ft long and elegantly arched escalator to the upper level – and you'll probably pause for a while. The view surpasses everything that Hamburg previously had to offer. Plus, if you're one of the lucky ones who managed to acquire a concert ticket you can take a seat in the main auditorium: none of the 2,072 seats in the 16 steeply climbing rows is more than

about 30 m/98.4 ft from the conductor. Connoisseurs love the (cheap) seats right at the top. The amazing sound of the Japanese acoustic specialist Yasuhisa Toyota makes this possible – a democratic way to enjoy music! *Platz der Deutschen Einheit 4 | www.elbphilharmonie.de/en | bus 111 Kaiserkai/Elbphilharmonie*

### 4 HAMBURG DUNGEON (132 C6) (*𝄞 L7*)

This is a kind of modern ghost train devoted to the history of Hamburg: from plague and fire to the cholera epidemic and an execution – all things gruesome, presented by actors in this combination of museum and theatre. A bit extreme and certainly not for children under 10 years of age. *Daily 10am–5pm | admission 23 euros | Kehrwieder 2 | tel. 040 36 00 55 20 | www.thedungeons.com/ hamburg/en | metro bus 6 Auf dem Sande*

### 5 INFOCENTER KESSELHAUS ● (133 D6) (*𝄞 L7*)

This is an ideal starting point for your tour through the old Speicherstadt and the new Hafencity, complete with café and lots of interactive stuff on the computer screens. The old power station that once served the Speicherstadt also has an 8×4 m/26.2×13.1 ft model of the city. Every Saturday at around 3pm free tours head from here through the real Hafencity. *Tue–Sun 10am–6pm, in summer Thu until 8pm | Am Sandtorkai 30 | tel. 040 36 90 17 99 | www.hafencity.com/en/ home.html*

Over a period of seven weekends in the summer, the square in front of the Infocenter is transformed into an open-air stage where the *Hamburger 'Jedermann'* (Everyman) is performed. Death arrives by boat, and Jedermann is a typical Hamburg 'moneybags' (merchant): a superb production against a stirring backdrop.

*Tickets 18–56 euros | tel. 040 3 69 62 37 | www.hamburger-jedermann.de | metro bus 6 Auf dem Sande*

### 6 INTERNATIONALES MARITIMES MUSEUM (133 E6) (*𝄞 M7*)

Built in 1879, the Kaispeicher B warehouse at the Magdeburger Hafen harbour is one of the oldest buildings in the Speicherstadt. You simply must have a look at the magnificently restored building. The extensive private collection of the former head of the Springer publishing company Peter Tamm, who died in 2016, is on display. He started collecting model ships when he was a young boy and assembled tens of thousands over the following decades, together with enormous oil paintings, uniforms, submarines and much more besides. Would-be captains can try the ship simulator: stand on the bridge steering your own giant container vessel through the port at Hamburg or Singapore. Not bad! *Daily 10am–6pm | admission 13 euros | Koreastr. 1 | www.immhh.de/internation al/en | bus 111 Koreastraße or Osakaallee (depending on direction of travel)*

### 7 LOHSEPARK (145 D–E6) (*𝄞 M7*)

Hafencity's green heartland is showcased in PR brochures – rather over-ambitiously – as a version of Central Park in New York. The large-scale U-Bahn station (Hafencity-Universität) with its cool light music concerts *(Sat/Sun, hourly)* certainly justifies this. But mainly families from nearby apartment buildings get together on the trampolines under the apple trees (a residents' association manages the apple harvest). There is even social housing here, while there are more day-care centres for children than in most of Hamburg's other districts. Many visitors also go to the new memorial at Hannover Bahnhof – this

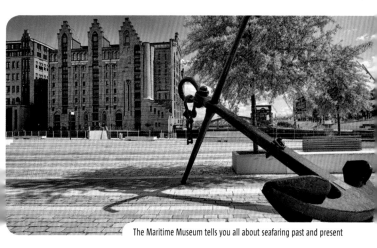

The Maritime Museum tells you all about seafaring past and present

was where the Nazis deported Jews and other Hamburgers to concentration camps ... *U4 Hafencity-Universität*

### 8 MAGDEBURGER HAFEN
(133 E6) (*M7*)

This is where Hafencity's 'brick-red heart' beats, as Hamburg's former Chief Planning Director Jörn Walter once put it. Carrying on from the Speicherstadt, bricks rule this area, in contrast to the 'white' Alster with its townsman's villas. Critics find it boring; even pirate Klaus Störtebeker looks down from his pedestal opposite the Korea-Brücke rather disdainfully onto the showy, tall arcades with their expensive restaurants. The *Headquarters of Greenpeace (Mon–Fri 9am–5pm | free admission | Honkongstr. 10/entrance via Elbarkaden)* at the end is definitely worth a visit. On the roof, wind turbines and solar panels generate the necessary energy; downstairs in the foyer there's an interactive exhibition on environmental and climate protection. *Bus 111 Koreastraße or Osakaallee (depending on direction of travel)*

### 9 MINIATUR-WUNDERLAND ★ ●
(132 C6) (*L7*)

A model railway that enjoys superlative after superlative, and rightly so. There is only one way to describe what the Braun brothers, together with their father and staff, have created in the Speicherstadt: a great experience for the whole family! The numbers are impressive: several hundred thousand figures, more than 10 km/6.2 mi of track, tens of thousands of wagons, vehicles, etc. It is the largest model railway in the world, operated by 64 computers – and the enthusiasm of the team. The Swiss Alps alone extend over three floors; you can see the Norwegian fjords and a gigantic airport with plains taking off and landing. Since the opening in 2001 there have been over 15 million visitors, more than to any other attraction in Hamburg. The best time to visit is early evening; you can INSIDER TIP book tickets in advance on the website and avoid the queues. And another tip: treat yourself to a tour behind the scenes. *Mon and Wed–Fri 9.30am–6pm, Tue 9.30am–9pm, Sat/Sun 8.30am–9pm (often open longer) | admission 12 eu-*

ros | Kehrwieder 2 | tel. 040 3 00 68 00 | www.miniatur-wunderland.com | metro bus 6 Auf dem Sande

### 10 OBERHAFENQUARTIER
(145 E6) (*M7*)

Where am I now? Most likely you're wondering this if you arrive from Hafencity. The large area (16.5 acres) behind the former railway maintenance depot is Hamburg's latest 'artists' quarter' – artists and creative types work in the old halls, sheds and warehouses. Don't be put off by what first looks like a rather run down area. The local chamber music association is a wonderful private initiative that organizes evening concerts (halle424.de). You can get hooked at the Hanseatische Materialverwaltung (a place that rents out almost everything!) (p. 75). *U4 Hafencity-Universität*

### 11 PROTOTYP (133 E6) (*M7*)

A museum for streamlined racing cars from the last 100 years, innovative sports cars, and elegant vintage specimens: this is not only where boyhood dreams become reality; cars also appeal to women – especially the beautiful ones! The racetrack simulator with an old Porsche convertible is great fun. *Tue–Sun 10am–6pm | admission 13.30 euros | Shanghaiallee 7 | www.prototyp-hamburg.de/en | bus 111 Koreastraße or Osakaallee (depending on direction of travel)*

### 12 SANDTORHAFEN (132 C6) (*L7*)

In good weather a pleasant place to go in Hafencity: a few lovely old ships and some sleek pontoons that are real technological marvels (underwater storerooms, swivelling, etc.). The Hamburg Maritime Foundation has invested a lot of time and effort into the project, mostly on a voluntary basis. Call by the harbourmaster's pavilion, which is usual-ly open, where they will gladly answer any questions. The INSIDER TIP historical photos on the railings leading up to the Sandtorkai are really interesting: take a look and compare with the scenes today! *Open 24 hours a day | free admission | metro bus 6 | bus 111 Am Sandtorkai*

### 13 SPEICHERSTADTMUSEUM
(132 C6) (*L7*)

There was a museum well before Hafencity had even been thought of. And indeed there's hardly a nicer attraction in Hamburg than this lovingly run museum, which showcases the working conditions of the quartermasters, the tea and coffee traders. *April–Oct Mon–Fri 10am–5pm, Sat/Sun until 6pm, Nov–March Tue–Sun 10am–5pm | admission 4 euros | Am Sandtorkai 36 | www.speicherstadtmuseum.de/english-summary.html | metro bus 6 Auf dem Sande*

### 14 SPICY'S (132 C6) (*L7*)

Viola Vierk has been a Speicherstadt enthusiast from day one. There wasn't much going on here when she first opened her spice museum in one of the old warehouses in 1993, but today it's a Hamburg institution. You can smell and taste exotic spices or participate in various informative events or offbeat walking tours. *Tue–Sun (July–Oct daily) 10am–5pm | admission 5 euros | Am Sandtorkai 34 | tel. 040 36 79 89 | www.spicys.de/en | metro bus 6 Auf dem Sande*

### 15 UNILEVERHAUS (144 D6) (*L8*)

From the outside, it looks like it has seen better days, but inside it's wonderfully chic. The multi award-winning office building is equipped with state-of-the-art sustainable technology and everything is vibrant, ergonomic and bright. The unobstructed views of the Elbe from the ☀ canteen terrace are unbeatable, though as a rule the canteen itself can only be used by employees. But the INSIDER TIP ice cream parlour with sun loungers is open to all and is a real treat. *Strandkai | U 4 Übersequartier*

## 16 VIEW POINT HAFENCITY ☀ (145 E6) (*M6*)

The orange tower has stood for many years in Hafencity, although it has moved around from time to time. Now and here, at the entrance to the Baakenhafen, it is sure to stay put for a few years to come, as it will be some time before this quarter is finished. Apartments are planned here, above all, but also a swimming pool, a park on an artificial island, houses on stilts above the water, etc., etc. ... It remains to be seen what will actually come to fruition.

There's definitely a fine view from the tower. *U 4 Hafencity-Universität*

# FROM ALTONA TO TEUFELS-BRÜCK

**Hamburg is one of the greenest cities in Germany. And right here, in the west of the city, you can see why this is the case. There's one beautiful park after another, and between them mansions and villas and of course the world-famous avenue, the Elbchaussee.**
But it isn't just the city's elite that has settled here. In places like Övelgönne

New buildings, old ships – Hamburg's mix at Sandtorhafen in Hafencity

many ordinary families continue to live even today, the descendants of captains and pilots who built their pretty houses along the banks of the Elbe. And Ottensen too offers something different: narrow streets, workers' houses, pubs, cafes, numerous shops and a beautiful cinema will tempt you to go on an extended shopping spree until well into the evening. Call in and see the Altonaer Museum. And, should you happen to get up early on Sundays, the Fischmarkt is open from 5am in summer.

## 1 ALTONAER BALKON ☼
### (143 E5) (∅ H7)

This is a great vantage point and a popular meeting place for boules players and barbecue enthusiasts. In the distance you can see the 500-m/1640-ft-long Köhlbrandbrücke, a bridge which spans the Köhlbrand shipping lane 54 m/177.2 ft above the water – still considered a technical masterpiece. The Altonaer Balkon is a good starting point for

## SIGHTSEEING FROM ALTONA TO TEUFELSBRÜCK
1 Altonaer Balkon
2 Altonaer Museum

Viewing terrace overlooking the harbour: Altonaer Balkon

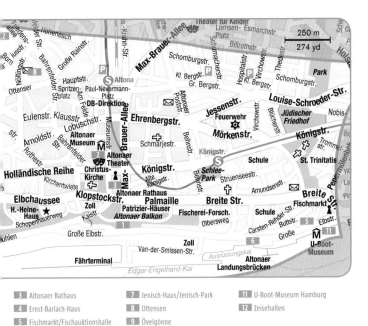

a walk. To the right, you can walk along the Elbe to Wedel in a couple of hours and, to the left, you can make your way into the city centre. Either way you'll be following the INSIDERTIP▶ Elbhöhenweg, a 23-km/14.3-mi path (not always signposted). *Palmaille/Klopstockplatz | bus and S-Bahn Altona*

### 2 ALTONAER MUSEUM
(143 E5) (*Ø H7*)

A well-run institution. When it was due for closure in 2010 due to lack of funds, a local action group organised protest sit-ins – and were successful. The museum stayed open and is being renovated. It has barges, old fish cutters and beautiful figureheads; model farmhouses and well-curated themed exhibitions. *Tue–Sun 10am–5pm | admission 7.50 euros | Museumstr. 23 |* *tel. 040 4 28 13 50 | www.altonaermuse um.de/en | bus and S-Bahn Altona*

### 3 ALTONAER RATHAUS (143 E5) (*Ø H7*)

'All to nah' to Hamburg (all too near), Altona was once a Danish city. For centuries it provided a home to many religious refugees, today still seen in the names of the streets such as 'Große und Kleine Freiheit' (great and small liberty). After the Second Schleswig War Altona became a part of Prussia in 1864. Between 1896 and 1898, the old terminus station was converted into a magnificent, white town hall with an equestrian statue of Kaiser Wilhelm I in front. Today it is one of the city's most popular registry offices. By the way, Altona only became part of Hamburg in 1937 with the so-called 'Greater Hamburg Act'. *Bus and S-Bahn Altona*

### 4 INSIDER TIP ERNST-BARLACH-HAUS
(141 F4) (*E6*)

This may be one of the nicest little museums in Hamburg. Werner Kallmorgen's modest building in the centre of Jenisch-Park is noteworthy for its clean lines. It now houses the magnificent collection of the Hamburg patron (and former tobacco magnate) Hermann F. Reemtsma. The sculptor Ernst Barlach was ostracised and persecuted by the Nazis but Reemtsma was undeterred and continued to give him commissions. *Tue–Sun 11am–6pm | admission 6 euros | Baron-Voght-Str. 50 a | tel. 040 82 60 85 | www.ernst-barlach-haus.de | metro bus 15 Marxenweg*

Once upon a time there was a station – Altonaer Rathaus

### 5 FISCHMARKT/FISCHAUKTIONSHALLE ● (143 F5) (*J7*)

It is a ritual end to a party or pub crawl in Hamburg to visit the *Fischmarkt* (fish market). It's a very entertaining experience with lots of colourful characters; the banter employed by the fruit and fish sellers may not be the politest but they put on a great show, and even by 6am there's usually a huge throng of visitors. As well as fish and seafood there are stalls selling fruit and vegetables, and the pot plants for 5 euros make a nice souvenir *(Sun, April–Oct 5am–9.30am, Nov–March 7am–9.30am)*. The best place to enjoy a Sunday brunch is in the *Fischauktionshalle* (auction hall), which was constructed by the Altona merchants in 1895 as a 'cathedral to fish'. *Bus 111 Fischauktionshalle*

### 6 GROSSE ELBSTRASSE
(143 E–F 5–6) (*H–J7*)

It has been quite a while now, since this street was notorious for kerb crawling. Today it's lined not by prostitutes and their clients but by one new building after another. The PR people call it a 'pearl necklace on the Elbe', though many of the 'pearls' remain empty. It's the same old story: glass, concrete and astronomical rents. Nevertheless a walk from the fish market to Övelgönne is interesting and there are a number of nice restaurants. Designed by architect Hadi Teherani, the ● ☆ INSIDER TIP *Dockland* is a spectacular office building, whose shape resembles a ship. You can climb the 140 steps onto the 'bridge' – the roof – where you'll be rewarded with sensational views. *S 1, 3 Königstraße | bus 111 Große Elbstraße*

### 7 JENISCH-HAUS/JENISCH-PARK ★
(141 F4–5) (*E6–7*)

Even at an early stage, the western part of Hamburg became the desired residential area for wealthy merchants. Jenisch-Haus is one of the most beautiful English-style mansions. Even Prussia's leading architect Karl Friedrich Schinkel was involved in the planning. The living rooms have been preserved in their original state and, today, form the core of the Museum of Art and Culture on the Elbe. *Tue–Sun 11am–6pm | admission 5.50 euros | reduced admission with the neighbouring Barlachhaus | Baron-Voght-Str. 50a | tel. 040 82 87 90 | metro bus 15 Hochrad.* The eponymous park was also laid out in the English style. In around 1800 Baron Caspar Voght had the land above the Elbchaussee developed into a model estate and at the same time created the landscaped park with views of the Elbe. There's a pleasant walk leading from the Teufelsbrück quay to the Loki-Schmidt-Garten, the botanical garden of the Hamburg University at the Klein Flottbek S-Bahn station.

Elegant interior: Jenisch-Haus

## ⑧ INSIDERTIP OTTENSEN
(143 D–E 4–5) *(𝄞 H6–7)*

This was always (and will hopefully long remain) Hamburg's liveliest district. The colourful mélange is unique in the city. Punks and pensioners, yuppies and eco-warriors, creatives and promoters – everyone lives here peacefully side by side. In Ottensen you can find some of the city's nicest restaurants, as well as unusual shops, delicatessens, cafés, fashion boutiques, pubs, Turkish snack stalls and trendy bars. For decades all attempts by estate agents and the property developers to harmonise the attractive hotchpotch by putting up boring new buildings have failed. *Bus and S-Bahn Altona*

## ⑨ ÖVELGÖNNE ★
(142 B–C5) *(𝄞 F–G7)*

In addition to Blankenese this is the most popular weekend destination for Ham-

burg's sun worshippers. The picturesque row of old captains' and ship pilots' houses on the banks of the Elbe is only a few hundred metres long. If you want to live here, you probably have to marry into one of the families; they guard their traditions tightly. That is why you should be discreet and not get caught pressing your nose too closely to the windowpanes. Don't miss a visit to the nowadays almost famous ● *Strandperle (Övelgönne 60 | daily in summer, Sat/Sun in winter and depending on the weather)*, a great beach bar right on the Elbe: feet in the sand, glass in your hand, watching the ships (and of course people) go by. You will find wonderful old ships in the *Museumshafen Övelgönne (free admission | www.museumshafen-oevelgoenne. de)*, and an old Hadag steamer has been converted into a café. If you see people pottering around there don't be afraid to INSIDER TIP speak to them, they're only too pleased to meet outsiders and to provide information. Under the glass dome on the roof of the Augustinum old age home is ⚜ *Café Elbwarte (Wed and Sat/Sun 3–6pm)*. The view is well worth it. A walk from here to Teufelsbrück takes about 90 minutes. *Bus 112 Neumühlen*

### ⑩ TEUFELSBRÜCK/ELBCHAUSSEE
### (141 F5) (*ⅅ D7*)

At Flottbek an der Elbe a stream once flowed into the Elbe river. The old bridge that crossed it was called the Teufelsbrücke (devil's bridge) after the neighbouring wooded area known as the Duwels Bomgarde, which, with its marshy lowlands, was considered to be a sinister place. The Count of Schauenburg, who once ruled in these parts, sold the land to a citizen of Hamburg; today the Teufelsbrück quay lies about halfway along Hamburg's most famous street, the Elbchaussee. In the days gone by, one went by horse and carriage on an outing to the 'Café zum Bäcker'; today, a convertible is the preferred mode of transport and one drinks one's espresso on the terrace of the famous *Louis C. Jacob* hotel (see p. 66, 92). The poet Detlev von Liliencron once called the Elbchaussee 'the most beautiful road in the world'. But for some time now the image of Hamburg's premier address has been severely dented. The traffic, especially on weekends with all the daytrippers, is terrible. In addition, uniform blocks of flats were thrown up in the old parks; some ugly, some pretentious, some both. And finally along came Airbus to the opposite bank of the Elbe, and from their expensive balconies residents now look straight across at the runway. How annoying! But the tourists were happy: when the A 380 first came in to land on the opposite side of the Elbe the Hotel Jacob was booked out! *Express bus 36, 39 | metro bus 21 | bus 286 | Hadag ferry 64 pier Teufelsbrück*

# FOR BOOKWORMS AND FILM BUFFS

**The Golden Glove** – The novel's title is named after the bar 'Zum Goldenen Handschuh' which is at Hamburger Berg. It's also true that the Fritz Honka, the ripper, was a regular guest here. Heinz Strunk researched the gruesome case of the 1970s, although all details may not be confirmed.

**A Most Wanted Man** – John le Carré switches to a post-Cold War scenario in this 2009 novel set entirely in Hamburg, involving the war on terror and plenty of spying and intrigue.

**The Beatles in Hamburg:** The Stories the Scene and How it All Began – Spencer Leigh's sensitive account conveys not only the story of the Beatles in Hamburg but also the whole spirit of the age (2011)

**Soul Kitchen** – Fatih Akin's 2009 comedy about a lovesick Greek cook from Wilhelmsburg. It is a real homage to Hamburg, the settings ranging from Le Canard Nouveau on the Elbchaussee to the Speicherstadt and out to the *Astra Stube* nightclub beneath the Sternbrücke

One of the nicest spots on the Elbchaussee: under the lime trees on the Hotel Jacob terrace

### ■ U-BOOT-MUSEUM HAMBURG
#### (143 F6) (*ℳ J7*)

It is a bit eerie, but very real: the 92-m/ 301.8-ft-long U-434 Russian submarine was launched in Nizhny Novgorod in 1976 and was operational all over the world as a spy vessel. It now occupies a prominent berth right by the Fischmarkt. If you are not claustrophobic, take a look inside. *Usually Mon–Sat 9am–8pm, Sun from 11am | admission 9 euros | St.-Pauli-Fischmarkt 10 | www.U-434.de | bus 111 Fischauktionshalle*

### ■ INSIDER TIP ZEISEHALLEN
#### (143 D4) (*ℳ H6*)

Dating from 1865, the former Zeise factory buildings, which produced ships' propellers, were converted in 1988 into a modern cultural centre incorporating a cinema, galleries, restaurants (such as the popular *Eisenstein*, p. 69) and the university's Institute of Theatre, Musical Theatre and Film. At the time the conversion of old industrial buildings was seen as a real innovation and became a model for many similar schemes in Hamburg. If you're interested you could, for example, make for the Otto-von-Bahren Park, where the enormous site of an old gas works has just been wonderfully transformed into living spaces. *Friedensallee 7–9 | metro bus 2 Friedensallee*

# GRINDEL-VIERTEL AND EPPENDORF

**The districts described here skirt the western bank of the Alster. The strip of greenery on the site of the former ramparts, Planten un Blomen, is the city's green lung.**

You can enjoy a beer with students at the university campus, learn about foreign cultures at the MARKK Museum am Rothenbaum, admire the Grindel tower

# GRINDEL-VIERTEL AND EPPENDORF

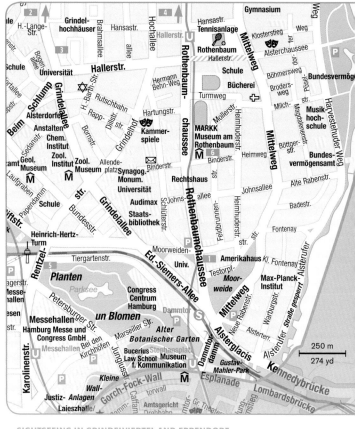

blocks and their place in Hamburg's architectural history or drink a glass of prosecco at one of the fashionable Italian bars in chic Eppendorf.

### ■ CAMPUS/STUMBLING BLOCKS
(144 C2) (*U5*)

The university is located in the Grindelviertel, where 40,000 students liven up the pubs and squares. Here you can also find Germany's oldest repertoire cinema (*Abaton*) and many lovely old town houses. Before World War II, Hamburg was home to more than 30,000 Jews, and one-third of them lived here in the Grindelviertel. The main synagogue was located on Bornplatz. It was destroyed by fire on the 'Night of Broken Glass' on 9 November 1938, from which time Jewish life in Grindel was systematically eradicated. Look out for the *'Stolpersteine'* (stumbling blocks), small brass plaques set into the pavement in front of the houses in remembrance of those who were deported and murdered. **INSIDER TIP** Hamburg's most famous chief rabbi Joseph Carlebach lived at Hallerstraße 76 until his deportation. *Grindelhof/Schlüterstraße | metro bus 4, 5 Grindelhof | U 1 Hallerstraße*

## 2 FALKENRIED-PIAZZA
### (136 B6) (*□ L3*)

Piazza? That sounds chic – just as chic as the apartments that have been built on the site of an old tram depot. Old and new have been tastefully combined here, and there are pubs and shops too. The adjacent Isebek Canal is a great place to relax and unwind. Some old workers' houses still stand between Löwenstrasse and Falkenried. The alternative appeal of their shared gardens and tenants' action groups makes them quite special! *U 3 Hoheluftbrücke, Eppendorfer Baum*

## 3 GRINDELHOCHHÄUSER
### (144 B–C1) (*□ L4*)

They were a real sensation: Hamburg's first postwar tower blocks. Each of the 12 blocks of flats is 200 m/656 ft long and they are described in the architectural lexicon as the 'reincarnation of the buried ideals of the 1920s'. In the nearby district office *(Grindelberg 66)* there is still an old **INSIDER TIP** paternoster lift in operation. *metro bus 5 Bezirksamt Eimsbüttel*

Popular inner-city residential area: charming old-style buildings in the Grindelviertel

**4 HAYNS PARK (136 C4) (🗺 L2)**

This is a delightful corner of Eppendorf with the Alster flowing by. It is said that the theatre director and film star Gustav Gründgens used to rehearse his roles in the small round temple here. In summer people compete for the best barbecue and picnic spots along the Alster, children splash around in the paddling pools and they all shoo the geese that – to put it delicately – leave their droppings all over the place. This is also the location of Hamburg's oldest boathouse, which has been a meeting place for canoeists ever since 1874: the *Bootshaus Silwar (Eppendorfer Landstr. 148 b | tel. 040 47 62 07 | www.bootshaus-silwar.com)*. If you want to try something different you can always rent a pedal boat in the shape of a swan *(boats from 10 euros per hour). Metro bus 20, 22, 25 Eppendorf Markt*

**5 MESSE/PLANTEN UN BLOMEN ●**
   **(132 B–C1) (🗺 L5)**

Hamburg's green lung – 'plants and flowers' in English – lies right next to the trade fair grounds, which have been extended as far as the TV tower. In the Middle Ages the ramparts were used to defend the city, but in the mid 19th century they were transformed into a green park. The greenhouses are a remnant of the days when this was Hamburg's only botanical garden. The new botanical garden is located in Flottbek, but with its plants, lakes and ponds, fountains, the Japanese garden, miniature golf and trampoline area, Planten un Blomen still has a lot to offer. It is wonderful to be able to relax on the wooden seats in the summer. There is an ice skating rink behind the *Hamburgmuseum* (see p. 38) that is used by inline skaters in summer; and there are playgrounds dotted around the park, the best one being on the corner of Marseiller Straße/St Petersburger Straße, (with pretty fountains). *May–Sept daily 7am–11pm, Oct–April 7am–9pm | www.plantenunblomen.hamburg.de | U 1 Stephansplatz | U 2 Messehallen*

**6 MARKK MUSEUM AM**
   **ROTHENBAUM (144 C2) (🗺 L5)**

This is one of the largest ethnological collections in Germany, and even the building, constructed in 1907–10, is impressive. The imposing entrance hall is

Idyllic garden at the foot of the television tower: Planten un Blomen

decorated with art nouveau features. The **INSIDER TIP** hall with masks from the South Seas is great – it's amazing to see what can be made out of grass and coconuts. And there's also a realistic-looking pharaoh's grave that you have to descend into. A family-friendly establishment. *Tue–Sun 10am–6pm, Thu 10am–9pm | admission 8.50 euros | tel. 040 4 28 87 90 | www.markk-hamburg.de | Rothenbaumchaussee 64 | U 1 Hallerstraße*

# MORE SIGHTS

## BALLINSTADT (149 F4) (*m O*)

A total of about 5 million people have left Hamburg for other parts of the world. Many of them spent their last weeks on German soil in the barracks of the so-called *Auswandererstadt* (emigration city) on the Veddel, which the former Hapag boss Albert Ballin had built at the end of the 19th century. Nothing here is that old, but the three halls have been reconstructed using the original plans. It's a very interesting museum with many details on the often tragic history of emigration. You can look for your forebears on a computer: all the passenger lists since 1840 are available. A pleasant – and appropriate – way to get there is with the **INSIDER TIP** Maritime Circle Line, whose launches call in at many stops around the harbour. Departure from the shipping piers *(pier 10 | day ticket 16 euros | tel. 040 28 49 39 63 | www.maritime-circle-line.de/englisch). Museum: daily 10am–6pm, Nov–March until 4.30pm (last admission one hour before closing) | admission 12.50 euros | Veddeler Bogen 2 | www.ballinstadt.de/en | S 3, 31 Veddel-Ballinstadt*

## INSIDER TIP HAFENMUSEUM
(149 D3) (*m M8*)

The harbour museum includes a floating steam crane, a dredger and an assortment of working vessels. In the shed there's an exhibition about dock working. From the end of the quay you look across to Hafencity. *April–Oct Tue–Fri 10am–5pm, Sat/Sun until 6pm | admission 5.50 euros | Australiastraße 50a | hafenmuseum-hamburg.de/en/home | S-Bahn 3, 31 Veddel-Ballinstadt, then bus 256 Hafenmuseum*

## JARRESTADT (137 F5) (*m N3*)

It's amazing: nowadays, hardly any architect would risk such a uniform design for a residential estate. But in the 1920s, Hamburg's building director Fritz Schumacher had other priorities – to plan dry, bright homes for affordable rents for the city's growing population. He succeeded in creating an attractive area. If you'd like to know more take a tour with the **INSIDER TIP** A-Tour's architecture experts *(group advance bookings: tel. 040 23 93 97 17 | a-tour.de/en/). Between Jarrestraße, Wiesendamm and Goldbekufer | bus 172 Jarrestraße*

## MUSEUM DER ARBEIT
(138 B5) (*m P3*)

Participation is what this labour museum is all about: on the premises of the former New York Hamburg Rubber Goods Company you (and your children) can get actively involved – in a printing shop, for example *(Mon 6pm–9pm)*. You can reach the museum by boat from Jungfernstieg *(April–Sept Sat/Sun three times per day | single journey 6.50 euros). Mon 1pm–9pm, Tue–Sat 10am–5pm, Sun 10am–6pm | admission 8.50 euros | Wiesendamm 3 | tel. 040 4 28 13 30 | www.museum-der-arbeit.de/en/en | S-/U-Bahn Barmbek*

### OHLSDORFER FRIEDHOF ★
(138–139 B–D1) (*ØØ O*)

The largest landscaped cemetery in the world is much more than just a final resting place for the dead – it is an excursion destination in its own right. The

The *Alte Land* keeps Hamburg in fresh fruit

benches under the large old trees are perfect for pondering over our worldly existence. The *crematorium (Fuhlsbüttelerstr. 756 | near the main entrance)* built by Fritz Schumacher between 1930–1932 is architecturally outstanding. One year later, Hamburg's building director was ousted by the Nazis. Many prominent Germans lie buried here and with 200,000 graves and an area of over 3.6 km²/900 ac, there is plenty to see. There is an information centre and a small museum. *April–Oct daily 8am–9pm, Nov–March 8am–6pm | main entrance Fuhlsbütteler Str. 756 | www.friedhof-hamburg.de/en/ohlsdorf-cemetery | S-/U-Bahn Ohlsdorf*

### INSIDER TIP ▶ SAMMLUNG FALCKENBERG (150 C4) (*ØØ O*)

This inspired collection of modern art is housed in an old tyre factory in Harburg. Something like this is normally only found in New York and naturally Berlin. A few of the rooms are taken up by the works of Jonathan Meese, and the private collection of Harald Falckenberg is now a satellite of the Deichtorhallen. *Guided tour only with prior booking, done via the website | admission/tour 15 euros | tel. 040 32 50 67 62 | www.sammlung-falckenberg.de/?site_language=EN | S 1, 31 Harburg Rathaus, then on foot*

### STADTPARK/PLANETARIUM ☼
(137 E4) (*ØØ N2*)

Fritz Schumacher also put his stamp on the Stadtpark (city park); the site was planned with military precision. The former hunting grounds of the landowner Adolf Sierich were to be transformed into an open-air 'house of the people' and that is what it remains to this day: on Sundays people gather on the large lawn to play sports, there's a beer garden, a natural swimming pool and an enormous playground. The INSIDER TIP ▶ Planetarium reopened in early 2017 after a refurbishment work. What was always wonderful – sitting back and gazing at the starry sky – is now even cooler. And finally, there is also a good café! *Entrance and observation deck Tue 9am–5pm (ticket office also Mon), Wed/Thu 9am–9pm, Fri 9am–10pm, Sat noon–10pm, Sun 10am–8pm, several shows daily | tickets from 11 euros | Hindenburgstr. 1 b | tel. 040 42 88 65 20 | www.planetarium-hamburg.de/en/home | U 3 Borgweg, then 10 min on foot*

## VOLKSPARKSTADION/HSV-MUSEUM (134 B–C5) (*O F3*)

You can get a good idea of the ups and downs of real fans of Hamburg's famous soccer team in the HSV Museum, and you can also book a tour of the stadium. *Daily 10am–5.30pm | admission 6, with tour 12 euros | tour daily at varying times | Sylvesterallee 7 | tel. 040 41 55 15 50 | www.hsv-museum.de/en | shuttle buses from S-Bahn stations Stellingen and Othmarschen for events only*

# TRIPS & TOURS

## ALTES LAND (150 A–B3) (*O O*)

When the apples blossom in the spring it's really gorgeous here. Altes Land is the largest single fruit-growing area in Northern Europe. In this case 'Alt' has nothing to do with the German word for 'old'. The first settlers here came from the Netherlands and 'Olland' was the original Low German name for this region. This gradually developed from 'olles Land' into 'Altes Land'. The small villages have charming names like Francop, Jork, Ladekop and Cranz and, with their houses built on dykes, they really are reminiscent of Dutch coastal villages. You can take lovely strolls along the dykes and look across the Elbe to Blankenese or Wedel; they are also ideal for skating or cycling along. A nice place to take a break is the *Obsthof Matthies (daily | Am Elbdeich 31 | tel. 04162 9 15 80 | www.obsthof.de)* just beyond Jork. And a great place to watch the boats and eat sausage is the *Lühe (Grünen Deich)* jetty, where cyclists congregate in the summer. *www.tourismus-altesland.de. By car or bike and ferry 64 from the Landungsbrücken to Finkenwerder, then a cycle tour as far as Steinkirchen*

## HARBURGER BERGE (150 C4) (*O O*)

It might be difficult to believe but there are also mountains around Hamburg and the restaurants are indeed called 'Berghütten' (mountain huts). Hamburgers come here to toboggan and even ski. The *Fischbeker Heide (S 3, 31 Neugraben, then bus 250 Fischbeker Heideweg),* is a wonderful area, with its moorland and hiking trails. If the children start whining, you can always continue to the *Wildpark Schwarze Berge (daily 8am–6pm, in winter 9am–5pm | admission 10 euros | Am Wildpark 1 | Rosengarten | www.wildpark-schwarze-berge.de),* home to wolves, lynx and bats and the comic potbellied pigs that grunt along behind you if you have brought food.

Right next door is the open-air museum *Freilichtmuseum Am Kiekeberg (Tue–Fri 10am–5pm | 9 euros | Am Kiekeberg 1/ Rosengarten-Ehestorf | www.kiekeberg-museum.de | S 3, 31 Neuwiedenthal, then bus 340 Wildpark or Museum Kiekeberg).* Here they do everything from threshing to baking bread – there's always something going on.

## SACHSENWALD (151 E–F3) (*O O*)

It was at *Schloss Friedrichsruh* castle in the Sachsenwald that the 'Iron Chancellor' Otto von Bismarck spent his twilight years. His descendants still live in the castle today. You can take some great walks here, visit two museums, the *Bismarck Museum (Tue–Sun 10am–6pm, Nov–March until 4pm)* and the *Bismarck Foundation (Tue–Sun 10am–6pm, Nov–Feb until 5pm | admission 4 euros | in the old station | www.bismarck-stiftung.de)* and the *Butterfly Garden (20 March–Oct 10am–6pm | admission 8 euros | www.garten-der-schmetterlinge.de)* and finally dine in style at the former training hall of boxer Max Schmeling: *Forsthaus Friedrichsruh restaurant (closed Mon | tel. 04104 6 99 28 99 | Budget). S 21 Aumühle*

# FOOD & DRINK

**The regional cuisine includes fish from the Elbe and the North Sea, fruit from the orchards of the Altes Land region and cabbage from Dithmarschen.**
Fortunately people in Hamburg like to eat well. Whether it's champagne soup, calamaretti or Barbary duck: the menus in the better restaurants in Hamburg leave nothing to be desired. As a result, Hamburg has (quite rightly) the reputation of being the best (even if not the cheapest) city in Germany for eating out. A willingness to try out new dishes and the influx of people from different corners of the world have both had an impact on Hanseatic tastes. Whether it's Italian, Viennese or Portuguese, everyone likes to try out new places here. And what really counts is a view of the Elbe or

Alster. For the privilege of dining along the river between the Fischmarkt and Övelgönne, for example, you will usually have to dig deeper into your pocket. The small bistros and snack bars where the chef in person does the cooking are usually very good. There is an abundance of such eateries in Ottensen, in the side streets of St Pauli or in the Karoviertel. For a long time now many chefs have used only regional and organic produce, and there are more and more vegetarian and vegan dishes to be found on the menus. At the top end of the scale you should definitely reserve a table well in advance – at least when it's the weekend. One tip for all those who enjoy good food: almost all top restaurants have excellent and moderately priced lunch

Photo: Restaurant Vlet

Plaice on the banks of the Elbe or a neighbourhood currywurst? Above all it's the view that's important in Hamburg!

menus. However, they are then usually closed for the afternoon. Cheaper restaurants provide hot meals throughout the day. Most cafés open at between 9am and 11am; the same goes for snack bars and bistros.

## CAFÉS & ICE CREAM PARLOURS

### ALEX HAMBURG ⋡ (133 D3) (𝄞 L6)
The café pavilion dating from 1953 is the seventh establishment at this location on the Binnenalster lake. During the Nazi period, Hamburg's young jazz musicians met here and opposed the regime. Today, guests are often loud but there is no jazz music. *Daily | Jungfernstieg 54 | tel. 040 3 50 18 70 | S-/U-Bahn Jungfernstieg*

### ALTONAS BALKON (143 E5) (𝄞 H7)
There is only one day when things aren't so idyllic at the garden café at Elbhöhenweg. During the Urbanathlon sporting event in July, athletes with rippling muscles almost jog right through the café. In winter, mulled wine and soups are

Tea weighing at Messmer Momentum

served. *Closed Mondays | Palmaille 41 | tel. 040 54 80 66 90 | S 1 Königstraße*

### INSIDER TIP BODO'S BOOTSSTEG ☼ (145 D2) (*M5*)
The nicest spot on the Alster: many people come to enjoy their lunch break in the deckchairs. Bodo Windeknecht looks after the boat hire while his daughter-in-law manages the café. *Daily, in winter weekends only | Harvestehuder Weg 1b/pier Rabenstr. | tel. 040 4 10 35 25 | bus 109 Böttgerstraße*

### CAFÉ KOPPEL ✆ (145 E4) (*N6*)
Late risers are in their element here, because they serve breakfast until 10pm. Everything is vegetarian, lots of it organic and the prices are fair. They open up the garden in summer. After a bite to eat you can take a stroll through the art and craft galleries of *Koppel 66. Daily | Lange Reihe 75 | tel. 40 24 92 35 | metro bus 6 Gurlittstraße*

### CAFÉ LEONAR ★ (144 C2) (*L4*)
One of the most interesting cafés in the city in the old Jewish quarter of Grindel. Kosher food, a cultural programme with Jewish emphasis, lots of magazines to read: the perfect place to think about life and everything else. Breakfast served daily until 3pm. *Daily | Grindelhof 59 | tel. 040 27 88 10 12 | metro bus 4, 5 Grindelhof*

### INSIDER TIP CAFÉ MIMOSA (144 A4) (*K6*)
Espresso, fresh brioche, friendly service and the day's newpapers: this little café near the Reeperbahn is a favourite spot for the residents of St Pauli. *Closed Mon/Tue | Clemens-Schultz-Str. 87 | tel. 040 32 03 79 89 | U 3 St Pauli*

### INSIDER TIP HERR MAX (144 A3) (*K5*)
The 'in' cake shop in the Schanzenviertel: the petits fours are decorated with skulls, some of the cakes with skeletons! Don't be put off – the delicious cakes and chocolates are freshly made on site in keeping with the best confectioners' tradition. Packed out at weekends. *Daily | Schulterblatt 12 | tel. 040 69 21 99 51 | U 3 Feldstraße*

### KONDITOREI LINDTNER (136 C5) (*L3*)
A wooden revolving door leads into the panelled elegance of this traditional German coffee shop; even ladies from posh Othmarschen come here for the Maharani gateau (with cognac) and the delicious homemade chocolates. Breakfast buffet at the weekend. *Daily | Eppendor-*

fer Landstr. 88 | tel. 040 4 80 60 00 | U 1, 3 Kellinghusenstraße

## KRÖGERS KLEINE SCHWESTER
(143 E4) (*ØD H6*)

'Kröger's Little Sister' is a café-bistro opposite the first inner-city branch of the furniture giant, IKEA, which is causing quite a stir: driving up rents on the one hand yet stimulating the retail landscape on the other. Watch developments for yourself over ginger tea and cake. You can buy coffee, tea and fine chocolates at *Kröger,* the coffee roaster's next door. *Closed Sun | Große Bergstr. 243 | tel. 040 36 02 83 08 | bus and S-Bahn Altona*

## MESSMER MOMENTUM
(132 C6) (*ØD L7*)

Teatime in Hafencity: in the lounge of Germany's largest tea importer you can enjoy a pot of Earl Grey with scones while looking out over the Sandtorhafen. The *tea museum (free admission)* provides a lot of interesting facts about the noble beverage. The shop stocks more than 150 blends. *Daily | Am Kaiserkai 10 | tel. 040 73 67 90 00 | bus 111 Magellan-Terrassen*

## DIE PATISSERIE (143 D4) (*ØD H6*)

Frenchman Pierre Ouvrard supplies Hamburg's luxury hotels with his tartes and baguettes. There is a 'no frills' small café in Ottensen with a welcoming French atmosphere. *Closed Mondays | Bahrenfelder Str. 231 | tel. 040 30 39 15 16 | bus 2 Gaußstraße*

## PUBLIC COFFEE ROASTERS
(132 B4) (*ØD L6*)

At the café in Neustadt filter coffee is expertly brewed with only five varieties on the menu. The coffee beans are rosted in Rothenburgsort. Every last Friday in the month *(7pm–9pm)* there is a tasting session of the dark brew at the **INSIDER TIP** *Public Cupping. Daily | Wexstr. 28 | mobile 0176 93 17 15 80 | S 1, 3 Stadthausbrücke*

## TRANSMONTANA (144 A3) (*ØD K5*)

Popular? This rather shabby looking place? Dead right! The Transmontana

---

⭐ **Café Leonar**
Read the newspaper, chat, and ponder: this kosher café is popular amongst the intellectuals of the Grindelviertel → p. 62

⭐ **Fischereihafen-Restaurant**
A classic among seafood restaurants – in a lovely location on the Elbe → p. 64

⭐ **Bullerei**
Popular: TV-chef Tim Mälzer's restaurant in the Schanzenviertel → p. 67

⭐ **Nil**
Trendy place with great food; youthful and lively → p. 69

⭐ **Schauermann**
Count the container ships going past from the retro 60s style chairs → p. 69

⭐ **Brooklyn Burger Bar**
Fabulous drinks – and pulled pork burgers to go with them → p. 67

⭐ **Louis C. Jacob**
One of the best chefs in the city and a personable host → p. 66

⭐ **Seven Seas Süllberg**
Beer garden and Michelin star restaurant with superb views from the banks of the Elbe at Blankenese → p. 66

**MARCO POLO HIGHLIGHTS**

on the Schanze is the grandmother of all Portuguese *galão natas* joints (that's milk coffee and custard tarts, plus other Portuguese specialities). No matter how worn out the chairs or how long the queue: this is where real insiders enjoy their *galão. Daily | Schulterblatt 86 | metro bus 15 Schulterblatt*

## SNACK BARS

**CURRY QUEEN DELI** (133 D5) (*ΩΩ M7*)
In keeping with the times, you can of course get vegan tofu sausages at this currywurst bistro, but the veal sausages go better with the excellent curry made with a hint of hibiscus or lemongrass. Served with Belgian chips – delicious! *Mon–Fri 11am–7pm | Zippelhaus 2 | tel. 040 76 75 76 26 | U 1 Meßberg*

**INSIDER TIP ESSZIMMER**
(144 A2) (*ΩΩ J4*)
Sooo tasty and sooo popular! The Esszimmer is one of the best lunches in town, and half of Eimsbüttel and the rest of Hamburg seem to know it. *Closed Sun | Eppendorfer Weg 73 | tel. 040 89 00 69 00 | metro bus 20, 25 Fruchtallee*

# FAVOURITE EATERIES

### How about fish? ...

Every Hamburger is familiar with this. When visitors arrive, guests politely ask during a city tour: where can we eat fish? Naturally, it shouldn't be too expensive and, if possible, spontaneous ... No problem! Fortunately, **INSIDER TIP** *Käpt'n Schwarz* (144 A–B5) (*ΩΩ K7*) (*daily | near St Pauli Landungsbrücken 6 | S-/U-Bahn Landungsbrücken | Budget)* has his snack bar selling fish rolls by the Alter Elbtunnel, so you can cross the quayside off the sightseeing list as well. If your guests have fussy children, then the go-to address is fish fryer's *Daniel Wischer* (133 D4) (*ΩΩ M7*) (*closed Sun | Große Johannisstr. 3 | tel. 040 36 90 19 88 | U 3 Rathaus | Budget)*. Hamburg's youngsters have enjoyed battered fish here for almost a century – and the chips also taste delicious. For a pleasant evening meal, everyone will get a warm welcome at *Fischerhaus* (144 A5) (*ΩΩ J7*) (*daily | Sankt-Pauli-Fischmarkt 14 | tel. 040 31 40 53 |* *bus 111 Pepermölenbek | Budget–Moderate)*. The lower dining room has seating capacity for up to 300 guests, although it's more pleasant on the upper floor with a fabulous view overlooking the docks. Slightly closer to the nightlife is *Elbfisch* (143 D5) (*ΩΩ H6*) (*daily | Bahrenfelder Str. 88 | tel. 040 39 90 92 77 | S-/U-Bahn Altona | Budget–Moderate)* in Ottensen. The appetizer plate with grilled octopus is a perfect summer snack and it's pleasant, though a little crowded, to sit outdoors.

### ... and fine dining

If there is time to enjoy restaurant service and the guests can afford it, then try the ★ *Fischereihafen Restaurant* (143 E6) (*ΩΩ H7*) (*daily | Große Elbstr. 143 | tel. 040 38 18 16 | bus 111 Fährterminal Altona | Expensive)*. Celebrities also enjoy dining at the Kowalke family establishment, and chef Rüdiger is now also part of the VIP scene. Ask for a window seat.

TV chef Steffen Henssler in his element – rolling sushi in Henssler & Henssler

### JIM BLOCK (133 D4) (*M L6*)

Without its Block restaurants many a Hamburg family would go hungry. The *Jim Block* line for the younger diner offers fast food of a high quality: steak and chips for the lads, baked potatoes and sour cream for the lasses. Always full. *Daily | Jungfernstieg 1 | tel. 040 30 38 22 17 | S-/U-Bahn Jungfernstieg*

**RESTAURANTS: EXPENSIVE**

### BROOK ⚘ (133 D5) (*M M7*)

The minimalist surroundings make a charming contrast to the superb view of the elaborate architecture of the Speicherstadt. Chef Lars Schablinski serves haute cuisine. *Closed Sun | Bei den Mühren 91 | tel. 040 37 50 31 28 | www.restaurant-brook.de | U 1 Meßberg*

### LE CANARD NOUVEAU ⚘
(142 C5) (*M G7*)

Simple and clear: at the gourmet temple on Elbchaussee (and possibly one of the best views over the River Elbe) there is no compulsory menu – the new chefs Florian Pöschl and Sebastian Bünning also love vegetarian cuisine. *Closed Sun/Mon | Elbchaussee 139 | tel. 040 88 12 95 31 | www.lecanard-hamburg.de | Metrobus 15 | Schnellbus 36 Hohenzollernring*

### CARLS (132 C6) (*M L7*)

Located in Hafencity, *Carls* is an offshoot of the *Louis C. Jacob* hotel restaurant on the Elbchaussee. Light snacks are available in the bistro at the front, complete with views of the Elbphilharmonie; in the chic restaurant at the back you can enjoy expensive dishes with views over the Elbe. *Daily | Am Kaiserkai 69 | tel. 040 3 00 32 24 00 | www.carls-brasserie.de/en | bus 111 Am Kaiserkai*

### HENSSLER & HENSSLER
(143 E6) (*M J7*)

Steffen Henssler is also a German TV chef. But his food is what counts: try the sushi rolls or tuna steak. The acoustics in the old warehouse, however, take some getting used to. *Closed Sun | Große Elbstr. 160 | tel. 040 38 69 90 00 | www. hensslerhenssler.de/en | bus 111 Sandberg*

### LOUIS C. JACOB ★ 🍴
(141 E5) (🗺 D6)

The city's No. 1 chef, awarded two Michelin stars, is Thomas Martin. The hotel restaurant has a dignified Hanseatic ambience and a lovely terrace in sum-

*Mon, evenings only | Bundesstr. 15 | tel. 040 4 10 75 85 | metro bus 4, 5 Staatsbibliothek*

### RIVE 🍴 (143 E6) (🗺 J7)

Rive was the first restaurant on this stretch of the Elbe to become popular with the trendy crowd. The most important question then and now: where do all the gorgeous waiters and waitresses come from? When it's full it does get a

Hearty fare at the old abbatoir: Tim Mälzer's Bullerei restaurant

mer overlooking the Elbe. Leave room for petits fours with your after-dinner coffee! *Closed Mon/Tue | Elbchaussee 401 | tel. 040 82 25 50 | www.hotel-jacob.de | express bus 36 | bus 286 Sieberlingstraße*

### LA MIRABELLE (144 B3) (🗺 L5)

The French chef is always in a good mood and the cheese trolley promises heavenly delights. Excellent little restaurant in the Grindelviertel. *Closed Sun/*

bit hectic. *Daily | Van-der-Smissen-Str. 1 | tel. 040 3 80 59 19 | www.rive.de | bus 111 Große Elbstraße*

### SEVEN SEAS SÜLLBERG ★ 🍴
(140 A5) (🗺 B6)

On the Süllberg in Blankenese it's not only the view that's exceptional, but also Karl-heinz Hauser's cuisine – worth two Michelin stars. Have a look in the ballroom and in summer visit the beer garden high above the Elbe. *Closed Mon/Tue (restaurant deck daily) | Süllbergter-rasse 12 | tel. 040 8 66 25 20 | express bus 48 Charitas-Bischoff-Treppe*

### THE TABLE (133 E6) (*M7*)

Hamburg's first three-star chef, a single large table which seats twenty guests and a menu for everyone – and all in the chic Hafencity. Gourmets queue up (for weeks) to dine at Kevin Fehling's restaurant. *Evenings only, closed Sun/Mon | Shanghaiallee 15 | tel. 040 22 86 74 22 | www.the table-hamburg.de | bus 111 Koreastraße*

### VLET (133 D6) (*M7*)

For some restaurant critics this is a real hotspot in the Speicherstadt/Hafencity area, for others it's just another example of how everything here is more chic and expensive. However, the fact remains that the food is good and the atmosphere in the old warehouse great. *Evening only, closed Sun | Am Sandtorkai 23, via the exterior spiral staircase | tel. 040 3 34 75 37 50 | www.vlet.de/en | bus 111 | metro bus 6 Am Sandtorkai*

## RESTAURANTS: MODERATE

### ATLAS (143 D3) (*H5*)

Old factory buildings with flair seem to attract good restaurants. That includes the Atlas in the Phoenixhof, a former industrial and commercial district in Ottensen. The great food and great atmosphere is complimented by the friendly staff. *Sat evenings only, Sun brunch only 10.30am–3pm | Schützenstr. 9 a (in Phoenixhof) | tel. 040 8 51 78 10 | metro bus 2 Schützenstraße (south)*

### BISTROT VIENNA (144 A2) (*K5*)

Can't be indiscreet here – the restaurant is tiny and everyone can hear every word – but that doesn't deter the regulars who come here to indulge in cod or boar ragout. No reservations so there may be a queue. *Evenings only from 7pm, closed Mon | Fettstr. 2 | tel. 040 4 39 91 82 | U 2 Christuskirche*

### BOBBY REICH (137 D6) (*M3*)

For generations those out for a stroll or 'to see and be seen' have been dropping in to eat here. The magnificent view over the Alster is uplifting, even if the drinks and homemade food are overpriced. *Daily | Fernsicht 2 | tel. 040 48 78 24 | bus 109 Harvestehuder Weg*

### BRASSERIE LA PROVENCE (143 D5) (*H6*)

Vive la France! Bright red walls, lavish décor and sumptuous food – tasty and cheerful. If you book you get an aperitif on the house. *Evenings only, closed Sun/Mon | Eulenstr. 42 | tel. 040 30 60 34 07 | metro bus 1 Große Brunnenstraße*

### BROOKLYN BURGER BAR ★ (143 D5) (*M7*)

Aspirin was the only thing you could buy here – now the super-friendly team in the old pharmacy at Domplatz serves burgers (vegan burgers too!) and amazing drinks. Jan and Steffen used to mix awesome drinks at the old Streit's cinema. This is a cool meeting place in the evenings – without a trendy beard and cheerful hat you will pleasantly stand out. *Daily | Alter Fischmarkt 3 | tel. 040 34 99 48 66 | brooklynburgerbar.de | bus 106 Brandstwiete/Rathausmarkt*

### BULLEREI ★ (144 A3) (*K5*)

Chef Tim Mälzer's establishment, in the brick halls of the old abattoir in Schanzen, is just to the taste of his trendy clientele. Tip: despite the crush you'll always find a seat in the cheaper deli section at the front. The food is whole-

# LOCAL SPECIALITIES

**Aalsuppe** – the aal here is Low German for 'everything' rather than Aal meaning 'eel'; so this is a typical soup made from leftovers, combining the sweet (prunes) with the savoury (bacon). If it does have real eel in it, then this is usually a concession to tourists

**Alsterwasser** – in other parts of Germany it's called *Radler*, in English shandy and that's exactly what it is: beer mixed with lemonade

**Birnen, Bohnen und Speck** – pears, green beans and bacon, together with potatoes, a kind of stew served in late summer

**Franzbrötchen** – tasty pastries with cinnamon, the perfect treat for a child that needs cheering up (photo right)

**Labskaus** – salted meat, beetroot, pickled herring, onions and potatoes passed through the mincing machine and with a fried egg on top. Come on, be brave! It tastes much better than it looks (photo left)!

**Scholle Finkenwerder Art** – generally speaking, these are large fillets of plaice, coated with breadcrumbs and served with fried bacon and sautéed potatoes. Still a Sunday favourite among locals

**Stinte** – a tiny species of salmon that, for a few years now, is found locally again in the Elbe and has become a yuppie speciality. Fried in flour, you eat it whole – head, tail and all. Only available during a few weeks in springtime

some and very tasty. *Daily, restaurant evenings only | Lagerstr. 34b | tel. 040 33 44 21 10 | www.bullerei.com | S-/U-Bahn Sternschanze*

### CAFÉ PARIS (133 D4) (*⍀ M7*)
For all lovers of French cuisine this is heaven! Of course all the waiters speak French, and the *steak frites* here really is *magnifique! Daily | Rathausstr. 4 | tel. 040 32 52 77 77 | U 3 Rathausmarkt*

### COPPER HOUSE (144 A5) (*⍀ K7*)
The large (it can seat 350 guests) Chinese restaurant has an open kitchen with 'live cooking' where you can see what's going on plus an all-you-can-eat self-service buffet. Plenty of fresh ingredients sourced locally. Difficult to imagine, but this always jam-packed place is still a down-to-earth, family-run business. *Daily | Davidstr. 37 | tel. 040 75 66 20 11 | S 1, 3 Reeperbahn*

### CUNEO (144 A5) (*∅ K7*)

Italian dishes have been served up in this family-run *trattoria* since 1905 – no frills, but as delicious as Mamma's home cooking. That seems to appeal to the media crowd, as to celebrities and tourists alike. *Evenings only, closed Sun | Davidstr. 11 | tel. 040 31 25 80 | S 1, 3 Reeperbahn*

### RESTAURANT ENGEL ⋇
(141 F5) (*∅ D7*)

Fantastic view of the ships sailing by from the Teufelsbrück quay. INSIDER TIP Sunday brunch. *Daily, Nov–Feb closed Tue | tel. 040 82 41 87 | Teufelsbrück pier, Elbchaussee | express bus 36 | ferry 64 Teufelsbrück*

### EISENSTEIN (143 D4) (*∅ H6*)

First opened in the 1980s when Ottensen was still down-at-heel. In the meantime, the district is almost as chic as this restaurant in the Zeisehallen. Delicious wood oven pizzas. *Daily | Friedensallee 9 | tel. 040 3 90 46 06 | metro bus 2 Friedensallee*

### MARINEHOF (132 C4) (*∅ L7*)

Indoors it's pretty hectic, but the restaurant in the gallery quarter on the Fleetinsel has a wonderful terrace. There's nothing better than sitting here in fine weather. *Closed Sun | Admiralitätstr. 77 | tel. 040 3 74 25 79 | S 1, 3 Stadthausbrücke*

### NIL ★ ⊚ (144 A4) (*∅ K6*)

Great organic cuisine in the hip atmosphere of an old shoe shop. And the kitchen staff never fails to come up with new ideas. *Evenings only, closed Tue | Neuer Pferdemarkt 5 | tel. 040 4 39 78 23 | U 3 Feldstraße*

### LE PLAT DU JOUR (133 D4) (*∅ M7*)

Jacques Lemercier, who once founded Hamburg's first gourmet restaurant, also has a more basic bistro: red tablecloths, good wines and very sensible prices, which explains why it's often full. *Daily | Dornbusch 4 | tel. 040 32 14 14 | U 3 Rathaus*

French bistro-style cuisine at the Café Paris

### SCHAUERMANN ★ ⋇
(144 A5) (*∅ K7*)

Regulars of the anarchist pub *Onkel Otto,* the flâneurs from *Park Fiction* and guests at the *Schauermann* all manage to coexist on this stretch of the Elbe where the Fischmarkt is. That the mixed neighbourhood functions at all is typical of Hamburg. The restaurant serves modern, light cuisine. *Closed Sun/Mon, evenings only | St.-Pauli-Hafenstr. 136 | tel. 040 31 79 46 60 | bus 112 St Pauli/Hafenstraße*

### SCHLACHTERBÖRSE (144 B3) (*∅ K5*)

The central meat market is next door, and so you tend to get big helpings on your plate; photos of celebrity guests

# RESTAURANTS: BUDGET

hang on the walls. *From 4pm, closed Sun | Kampstr. 42 | tel. 040 43 65 43 | U 3 Feldstraße*

### STRICKER'S 🌿 (132 B6) (*Ⓜ L7*)
The restaurant with an international reputation is at the Kehrwiederspitze, almost on the lower level of the Elbphilharmonie. You can hear the ships docking at the landing jettys, and the view is almost better than from the concert hall above. *Daily | Am Sandtorkai 7 | tel. 040 51 90 30 61 | bus 111 Am Kaiserkai*

## LOW BUDGET

A reasonably priced lunch and theatre atmosphere is provided by *Die Kantine* **(133 F3)** (*Ⓜ M6*) *(Mon–Fri 11.30am–3pm | Kirchenallee 39 | tel. 040 24 87 12 73 | S-/U-Bahn Hauptbahnhof)* in the Schauspielhaus. Guests eat in the front room while the rear is reserved for the ensemble.

At *Pizza-Bande* **(144 A5)** (*Ⓜ J7*) *(daily | Lincolnstr. 10 | www.pizza-bande. de | S 1, 3 Reeperbahn)* in St Pauli, the chefs swirl the pizza dough through the air and invent wild creations, e.g. Tandoori and pumpkin pizza. A simple Margherita costs about 6 euros; you can choose other toppings from the menu.

The *Bistro in den Rathauspassagen* **(145 D5)** (*Ⓜ M6*) is sponsored by the Diakonie charity. Its concept: fair, sustainable, public spirited. Soups or quiche from 2.20 euros. *Mon–Fri from 8am, Sat from 9am, closed Sun | Rathausmarkt | steps down to S- and U-Bahn station Jungfernstieg*

### WASSERSCHLOSS (133 E5) (*Ⓜ M7*)
The building was formerly the workplace of people who serviced and repaired the warehouse winches, but architects with vision originally designed this as a small castle. Now it houses an extraordinary restaurant and absolutely amazing teashop. Just one of their specialities is tea-smoked fish. Nice Sunday brunch (booking essential). *Daily | Dienerreihe 4 | tel. 040 5 58 98 26 40 | U 1 Messberg*

## RESTAURANTS: BUDGET

### BADSHAH RESTAURANT (133 F3) (*Ⓜ N6*)
A basement restaurant in St Georg, just near Hansaplatz – normally not such a fine Hamburger address. But the small restaurant with vibrant Bollywood memorabilia on the walls is an exception. Delicious Indian specialities are served for less than 10 euros. *Daily | Bremer Reihe 24 | tel. 040 24 60 43 | S-/U-Bahn Hauptbahnhof*

### BAREFOOD DELI (133 E3) (*Ⓜ M6*)
Occasionally, he shows up – the restaurant owner himself, Till Schweiger. Downstairs, you can enjoy hearty food like cheeseburgers, pasta or lentil soup. Upstairs, the enterprising actor and director sells plates, bed linen and other products in his furnishings shop. *Closed Sun | Lilienstr. 5–9 | tel. 040 36 93 05 40 | S-/U-Bahn Hauptbahnhof*

### ELBFAIRE 🌐 (133 E6) (*Ⓜ M7*)
The ingredients for the tasty dishes are all fair trade produce, mostly organic and primarily vegetarian cuisine. The building also houses the *Ökumenisches Forum,* so menus inspired by chefs at the monastery canteen are also available. You are welcome to look at the small

Packs a punch – the Oberhafen-Kantine on the edge of the Speicherstadt

chapel next door – but don't worry, saying prayers at table is not compulsory here. *Closed Sun | Shanghaiallee 12 | tel. 040 3 69 00 27 83 | bus 111 Koreastraße*

### ERIKAS ECK (144 B3) *(ⓜ K5)*
The opening times – INSIDER TIP warm meals from 5pm to 2pm! – might be a reason why night owls, early birds and taxi drivers find their way here for their meat loaf or steak; the huge *schnitzel* is another. *Sat/Sun only until 9am | Sternstr. 98 | tel. 040 43 35 45 | U 3 Feldstraße*

### INSIDER TIP OBERHAFEN-KANTINE (133 F6) *(ⓜ M7)*
The brick building under the bridge leans alarmingly to one side. But it's nothing to worry about; the building dating from 1925 is solid enough. The former 'people's coffee hall' is a protected building and tempts diners with dishes such as Labskaus with quail egg and rollmop. *Daily | Stockmeyerstr. 39 | tel. 040 32 80 99 84 | www.oberhafen kantine-hamburg.de | U 1 Meßberg*

### PONTON OP'N BULLN ☀
(140 B4) *(ⓜ B7)*
'Bulln' is what the residents of Blankenese call their quay. The snack bar there serves salmon cakes, soups and other goodies and is cheaper than the restaurant at the other end of the jetty. It's cosy inside in the winter. *Daily, Nov–Feb Thu–Sun only | Strandweg, Blankenese pier | tel. 040 86 64 51 27 | express bus 48 Blankenese/ferry*

### TH2 (136 B6) *(ⓜ L3)*
Light, bright and only slightly overpriced. The stylish bistro goes well with elegant Winterhude. Their breakfast served with a good choice of teas is excellent. *Daily | Klosterallee 67 | tel. 040 42 10 79 44 | U 3 Hoheluftbrücke*

### TI BREIZH (132 C5) *(ⓜ L7)*
Pure Brittany with crêpes and cider. In summer they have tables on the pontoon on the Nikolaifleet. They also have a little shop selling Brittany-style fisherman's shirts. *Daily | Deichstr. 39 | tel. 040 37 51 78 15 | U 3 Rödingsmarkt*

# SHOPPING

**CITY WHERE TO START?**

Hamburg's main shopping streets, Spitalerstraße and Mönckebergstraße with their department stores and clothing chains begin around 50 metres from the Hauptbahnhof and extend all the way to the Rathausmarkt. All around the Rathaus things get more Hanseatic and stylish and you'll find some beautiful traditional shops next to famous brands. From there you can stroll along the flagship addresses of the Große Bleichen or the Neuer Wall towards the Jungfernstieg.
*S-/U-Bahn Jungfernstieg*

**Shopping in Hamburg is a lot of fun, whether in the heart of the city or in the lively surrounding districts.**

All around the Jungfernstieg and the Gänsemarkt, in the Hanseviertel and the Hamburger Hof you'll find exclusive haute couture and jewellery shops. Department stores and cheaper shops are located towards the Hauptbahnhof. And small, quality shops you will find along the city's side streets, e.g. around Poolstraße near the Laieszhalle, where bespoke tailors and young designers offer their wares for sale. Each district has its own shopping area. There are numerous shops along the exclusive Eppendorfer Baum and the Lange Reihe in St Georg, where alongside established businesses, more and more lingerie and label shops are opening up

A sailor shirt or a designer gown? Hamburg is a shopper's paradise where you can have your every wish fulfilled

and window-shopping is a lot of fun. In Ottensen, in the Schanzenviertel and in Winterhude there is an unbelievable variety of fashion boutiques, delicatessens and specialist outlets. The top address for fashion 'made in Hamburg', vinyl records and quirky artisan shops like *Lockengelöt* (see p. 75) is the Karolinenviertel (Karoviertel for short) and Marktstraße. In the city centre shops are usually open until 8pm, smaller shops may close earlier. On the Reeperbahn shopping can also be done at night.

## DELICATESSEN

**BONSCHELADEN** (143 D4) *(𝄞 H6)*
Homemade sweets with strawberry, ginger or liquorice flavour; INSIDER TIP exquisite cream caramels, which are made before your eyes. *Closed Mon | Friedensallee 12 | bus and S-Bahn station Altona*

**HUMMER PEDERSEN** ⭐
(143 F6) *(𝄞 J7)*
Joachim Niehusen is passionate about seafood, and he passionately sells his

Trendy furniture and accessories at Stilwerk on Fischmarkt

lobster and fish, whether in his shop or the stylish bistro. INSIDER TIP If you arrive before 2pm, then you can admire the fresh daily catch. *Mon–Fri 6am–2pm, Sat until 10pm, Bistro Mon–Thu noon–6pm, Fri/Sat until 10pm | Große Elbstr. 152 | bus 111 Sandberg*

### KAREN'S KONDITOREI
(144 B1) (*ⓜ K4*)
Tiny family business, but Hamburg connoisseurs know that this is where you get some of the best cakes and croissants in the city. *Closed Mon, Sat/Sun only until 1pm | Beim Schlump 14 | metro bus 5 Bezirksamt Eimsbüttel*

### KARSTEN HAGENAH (143 D2) (*ⓜ G4*)
The new premises are spacious and tiptop: A huge selection of fresh fish, crab salad and smoked fish to take away and fried fish in the bistro. *Mon–Wed 7am–4pm, Thu/Fri 7am–6pm, Sat 7am–2pm | Schnackenburgallee 8 | bus 180 Winsberg (south)*

### MUTTERLAND (133 F3) (*ⓜ M6*)
Here you can buy German delicacies. The shop and café are located at the Hauptbahnhof, so it's perfect for shopping travel supplies and souvenirs, such as INSIDER TIP the Kakao Kontor chocolate from Eimsbüttel. A word of caution: they might look really nice but some of the goods are overpriced. *Café also open Sun | Ernst-Merck-Str. 9 | S-/U-Bahn Hauptbahnhof*

### RINDERMARKTHALLE ⭐
(144 A4) (*ⓜ K6*)
The top floor is home to a number of clubs, a mosque and the Dom Kindergarten; in the main hall, more than 20 small shops and snack stands offer their wares. Something is always going on here – in winter curling, in summer food trucks and flea markets. Try the INSIDER TIP drinking chocolate at Confiserie Paulsen, an old, established Hamburg company which still makes its own pralines. *Neuer Kamp 31 | U 3 Feldstraße*

### K. W. STÜDEMANN (144 A3) (*ⓜ K5*)
Nostalgic shop in the Schanzenviertel. Despite the chichi clientele, the locals still keep coming to this chocolatier for the very best biscuits, tea and coffee. *Schulterblatt 59 | metro bus 15 Schulterblatt*

## WEINKAUF ST GEORG
(145 E4) (*M N6*)

The shop's own 'St-Georg' sparkling wine is the bestseller. Schnapps and oil is bottled straight from the carafe. During wine tasting the owners are happy to tell visitors about the district. *Lange Reihe 73 | S-/U-Bahn Hauptbahnhof*

FURNISHINGS ETC.

## CUCINARIA
(136 B5) (*M L3*)

In Eppendorf's specialist cook shop even an egg separator is available as an essential kitchen gadget and stylish accessory. You can buy about 6000 kitchen items and cooking accessories here. *Straßenbahnring 12 | U 3 Hoheluftbrücke*

## HÄNGEMATTENLADEN
(143 D5) (*M H6*)

The name means 'the hammock shop'. Net hammocks, family-sized hammocks, hanging chairs and even **INSIDER TIP** hammocks for babies. Not expensive and with competent sales assistants. *Bei der Reitbahn 2 | bus and S-Bahn station Altona*

## LOCKENGELÖT
(132 A2) (*M K6*)

Wonderfully eccentric: toilet roll holders made from vinyl records, a bar from oil barrels and key racks made from old books. A visit to the shop is an experience in itself. *Marktstr. 114 | U 3 Feldstraße*

## STILWERK ● (143 F5) (*M J7*)

The old maltings at the Fischmarkt is home to seven floors of exclusive brands, from designer lights to kitchens to upholstered furniture. And even if you don't have the money, window-shopping here can be inspiring. *Große Elbstr. 68 | bus 111 Fischauktionshalle*

## LOCAL SPECIALITIES

## BUDDEL-BINI (137 D4) (*M M2*)

The Binikowski family has sold ships in bottles for more than 30 years, a business that's now run by the second generation. Good online shop. *Barmbeker Str.171 | www.buddelbini.de | U 1 Hudtwalckerstraße*

## ERNST BRENDLER (133 D4) (*M M7*)

Naval and maritime uniforms as well as tropical clothing specialist. The venerable shop has been in business since 1879 and still retains a hint of the colonial era. *Große Johannisstr. 15 | U 3 Rathausmarkt*

## HANSEATISCHE MATERIALVERWALTUNG
(145 E6) (*M M7*)

A cooperative shop that sells or rents out old theatre and film props. The old warehouse in the Oberhafen area of Hafencity is worth a visit just because of

★ **Hummer Pedersen**
Seafood can't get any fresher: traditional fishmonger → p. 73

★ **Rindermarkthalle**
Great mix of neighbourhood culture and supermarket with a difference → p. 74

★ **Isemarkt**
Germany's longest market, sheltered from the rain under an elevated railway line → p. 76

★ **Fahnen Fleck**
Angels' wings, national flags, long-haired wigs for rocker sessions: you'll find it all here! → p. 78

MARCO POLO HIGHLIGHTS

# MARKETS

the location. *Mon–Fri 2pm–6pm, longer in summer | Stockmeyerstr. 41–43 | U 1 Steinstraße*

## MARKETS

### FLEA MARKETS
In the flea market season there is always a market going on in some district at some time. Check the local papers or *hamburg.de/flohmarkt* for info.

### WEEKLY MARKETS
Arguably the most attractive but undeniably the longest weekly market in Germany is ★ *Isemarkt (Tue, Fri 9am–2pm)*: the fruit, vegetable and cheese stall-holders spread out their wares under the elevated railway line between Hoheluftbrücke and Eppendorfer Baum (U3). A must for those with a sweet tooth is INSIDER TIP Bonbon Pingel with biscuits and liquorice for everyone to try. Each district has its own weekly market, with a total of around 100 in Hamburg. Look in the local press for times or at *www.hamburger-wochenmaerkte.de*. And for those who can't get enough during the day: every Wednesday *(4pm–11pm, Nov–March until 10pm)* there is an atmospheric INSIDER TIP night market that takes place on Spielbudenplatz *(Reeperbahn | U 3 St Pauli)*.

## ELEGANT FASHION

### LADAGE & OELKE (133 D4) (𝄞 L6)
The traditional local prefers to dress like an Englishman: duffle coat, blazer, muted colours, dignified, discreet. That's exactly what you'll find here, where that tradition continues. *Neuer Wall 11 | S-/U-Bahn Jungfernstieg*

### POLICKE (145 F4) (𝄞 N6)
Here there's no such thing as 'it doesn't suit you'! There's an enormous and reasonably priced choice of mostly classic menswear, and the closely packed rows of suits extend over several floors. *Böckmannstr. 1a | S-/U-Bahn Hauptbahnhof*

Classy weekly market: the Isemarkt under the elevated railway

**VATER & SOHN** 🌐 (144 A2) (*🗺 K4*)
Handwoven original jeans (also for women), shirts made from wild cotton, genuine leather belts – the clothes cost more here than elsewhere, but they last for ages and producers are paid a fair wage. *Eppendorfer Weg 54 | U 2 Christuskirche*

**WÄSCHEHAUS MÖHRING** (132 C4) (*🗺 L6*)
In this venerable establishment you will find an impressive selection of linens, nightwear and underwear. Established in the heart of the city for more than 200 years. *Neuer Wall 25 | S-/U-Bahn Jungfernstieg*

## TRENDY FASHION

**HARD ROCK CAFÉ** (144 B5) (*🗺 K7*)
Firstly you find them in many other cities, secondly it is a popular place to eat, and thirdly they sell their world famous tops, jewellery and accessories. Three good reasons why the place is always packed! *St Pauli Landungsbrücken, Brücke 5 | U- and S-Bahn Landungsbrücken*

**HERR VON EDEN** (132 A2) (*🗺 K6*)
Herr von Eden, alias Bent Angelo Jensen, has long supplied distinctive and elegant outfits for fashion-conscious men and women, including Lady Gaga and Depeche Mode. Well known for his stylish and impeccably made bespoke suits. *Marktstr. 33 | U 3 Feldstraße*

**SHIRTLAB** (132 A2) (*🗺 K6*)
Hoodies, T-shirts, tanktops – you name it, they'll print it here with a host of crazy or chic designs, or even to your own specifications. *Marktstr. 16 | U 3 Feldstraße*

**WIE ES EUCH GEFÄLLT**
(144 A3) (*🗺 K5*)
Boutique stocking the imaginative and playful creations of young fashion designers, from jersey dresses and blouses to jewellery and stylish accessories. *Juliusstr. 16 | S-/U-Bahn Sternschanze*

## MUSIC

**HANSEPLATTE** (144 B4) (*🗺 K6*)
This trendy record shop right next to the old abattoir sells music made by Hamburg-based artists and labels such as Kettcar and Tocotronic, as well as some unusual souvenirs and clothes. Readings and concerts are also held here. *Neuer Kamp 32 | www.hanseplatte.de | U 3 Feldstraße*

**JUST MUSIC** (144 B4) (*🗺 K6*)
Professionals and amateurs alike can find everything they need in this music shop in a bunker on the Heiligengeistfeld, from electric bass and violins to DJ equipment or drumsticks. And you can try out almost every instrument. *Feldstr. 66 | in the Hochbunker | U 3 Feldstraße*

**MICHELLE** (133 E4) (*🗺 M6*)
In Hamburg's 'only true' record shop, bands regularly give INSIDER TIP▶ concerts in the window. Flyers give details about the best gigs in town. *Gertrudenkirchhof 10 | U 3 Mönckebergstraße*

## SHOPPING ARCADES

● Believe it or not, there are 13 shopping arcades in central Hamburg and the Stadthöfe at the Neuer Wall is their most recent addition. Theoretically you could shop all day between Gänsemarkt and Hauptbahnhof (main railway station) without feeling a single drop of rain. The *Europa-Passage* (133 D4) (*🗺 M6*), designed by Hamburg's favourite architect Hadi Teherani, is the largest shopping mall in the city. It is a five-storey palace of consumerism (from the top you have a superb view over the Binnenalster) with glass lifts, shops, fast food outlets and even an art gallery displaying works by Germany's aging rocker Udo Lindenberg. Whether for people watching or more exclusive shopping, the locals also like going to *Galleria* (132 C4) (*ɰ L6*), where a French bistro serves café au lait or champagne to go with the view over the canal. Architects also succeeded in converting the *Levantehaus* (133 E4) (*ɰ M6*), a 100-year-old *Kontorhaus* office building on Mönckebergstraße, into a chic shopping arcade with small outlets.

## SHOES & BAGS

**FREITAG** (133 F4) (*ɰ M7*)
The trendy Swiss cult label stocks the original as well as solid bags made from recycled truck tarpaulins. *Klosterwall 9 | S-/U-Bahn Hauptbahnhof*

**KLOCKMANN** (132 C3) (*ɰ L6*)
One hundred years ago Ernst Klockmann began designing cases. If you have some money left over, do consider having a INSIDERTIP 'Hamburger Beutel' (Hamburg bag) made, finished off to your own specifications – with magnetic snap or zip closure and lining of your choice. *Gänsemarkt 50 | Gänsemarktpassage | U 2 Gänsemarkt*

**SCHUH MESSMER** (144 A5) (*ɰ K7*)
The oldest shoe store in the city now offers shoes with some very high heels. Men come here for their snakeskin ankle boots and thigh high boots that are available in extra large shoe sizes. *Also Sun 2pm–8pm | Reeperbahn 77–79 | S 1, 3 Reeperbahn*

## SPECIALIST SHOPS

**FAHNEN FLECK** ★ (132 C3) (*ɰ L6*)
This shop is as much a part of Hamburg as St Michael's church tower: carnival costumes, masks, fireworks and the full range of national flags. *Valentinskamp 30 | U 2 Gänsemarkt*

**GLOBETROTTER** (138 B5) (*ɰ P3*)
The more exotic the destination and mode of travel, the more attentive the service: this magnet for all outdoor enthusiasts is located in a bright red cube at Barmbek station. There's a climbing wall and a walk-in refrigerator for testing specialist equipment. *Wiesendamm 1 | S-/ U-Bahn Barmbek*

**GUTE JACKE** (133 E6) (*ɰ M7*)
You might not think it, but Hafencity has some nice little independent shops. This one sells jackets for your walk along the

Elbe or your next visit to the Alps. Good service. *Überseeboulevard 3 | U 4 Überseequartier*

## MEISTER PARFÜMERIE
(136 C6) (*M L3*)

Unusual scents for refined senses! A genuinely beautiful shop, which has remained in family ownership since 1888. *Eppendorfer Baum 12 | U 1 Klosterstern*

## NADELHEIM (133 E4) (*M M6*)

The finest felt in town: Felicitas and Fabian Leske turn thick wool felt into attractive items at their small shop in the Levantehaus. They even sew to order. You can watch as bags, hot water bottle covers or baby booties are made and embroidered. *Mönckebergstr. 7 | S-/U-Bahn Hauptbahnhof*

## NIVEA-HAUS (133 D3) (*M L6*)

Nivea comes from Hamburg – so what could be more appropriate than taking home a blue tin as a souvenir? Or treat yourself to a massage in the spa (from 95 euros). *Jungfernstieg 51 | tel. appointment 040 82 22 47 40 | S-/U-Bahn Jungfernstieg*

## PAPPNASE & CO (144 C2) (*M L5*)

Enough to make anyone smile: balls for juggling, red noses, complete clown outfits and makeup; an international comic shop can be found next door. *Grindelallee 92 | metro bus 4, 5 Grindelhof*

## REDGALLERY (132 C5) (*M L7*)

Gem stones, jewellery, minerals, fossils – plenty of kitsch and the occasional dinosaur skeleton. This unique gallery specializes in nature products and is like a mix of museum and bazaar. If you're lucky, mammoth horns or a giant clam will be on offer as home decorations. *Rödingsmarkt 19 | U 3 Rödingsmarkt*

Shopping under cover: Europa-Passage

## SCHIRM & CO (133 E4) (*M M6*)

This umbrella shop is a Hamburg institution and they are also open longer on rainy days. The Vertein family also provides a repair service for broken umbrellas. *Rosenstr. 6 | S-/U-Bahn Hauptbahnhof*

## STEGMANN (133 D3) (*M L6*)

Shank buttons, ordinary buttons, rhinestone or velvet buttons or those with leather and mother of pearl – the collection inside Germany's only specialist buttons store is amazing. Women's fashion, scarves and other accessories are also available. *Jungfernstieg 46 | U 2 Gänsemarkt*

## THE ART OF HAMBURG
(132 A5) (*M K7*)

The 'Machinist' T-shirts with real oil stains (not guaranteed to come out) have cult status and are a tribute to the nearby port, as are the hoodies with maritime logos. All around the side streets of the Portuguese district you can find other nice shops. *Ditmar-Koel-Str. 19 | S-/U-Bahn Landungsbrücken*

# ENTERTAINMENT

**CITY** **WHERE TO START?**
Nightfall in Hamburg: it's always the **Reeperbahn (144 A5)** (*⟨⟨⟩ J–K 7*) that comes to mind and it is also the destination of Hamburg's youth at every weekend. It is where the best clubs and bars are, and it's also just a stone's throw from the other trendy area of the Schanzenviertel. It's simply the place to go. Even culturally minded people are well catered for: from musicals to theatre to cabaret. If it's too crowded for you and you'd just prefer a leisurely beer, almost all districts of the city have their own nightlife.

First the good news: Hamburg's nightlife is easy to get the hang of. St Pauli, the Schanzenviertel, Ottensen and St Georg – the real revellers' hotspots – can readily be navigated by public transport.

But that's about as far as the prescription for a good night out can go, simply because the scene is so varied. St Pauli has the important live music clubs, the trendy bars and discos, cheek by jowl with dimly lit pubs and amusement arcades. Go with the flow and visit places where the atmosphere looks good, such as around Hans-Albers-Platz or the Hamburger Berg for example. This is where you'll find young people, Hanseatics and tourists all dancing and real dive bars. In the summertime the Elbe beach be-

## The main entertainment area is the Reeperbahn – but there's plenty of nightlife in other parts of the city as well

tween Neumühlen and Teufelsbrück is one big open-air pub. They barbecue and chill out and the restaurants are all packed. Ottensen has more pubs than clubs, and here too on warm summer evenings you sit outside, even if it's just with a can bought from the local kiosk. In the Schanzenviertel the popular spots are the Schanzenpiazza opposite Rote Flora and neighbouring streets. Night owls can find more and more trendy bars towards St Pauli: along the pedestrian area from the Schulterblatt via Neuer Pferde-

markt and Wohlwillstraße, new bars and pubs open every month. The Lange Reihe in St Georg is where touts, theatregoers and the gay scene congregate. Out towards Steindamm prostitution and drug dealing represent the seamier side of the city's nightlife. Hafencity is one district that has not yet developed any real nightlife of its own: there are cafés but that's about it.

Hamburg offers an exciting cultural and theatre scene, and a prize-winning fringe scene *(www.hamburg-off.de)*. Elb-

Classy and incredibly stylish with an excellent bar: Die Bank

philharmonie, Staatsoper Hamburg (opera house), Schauspielhaus (theatre) and Thalia-Theater are among the leading such institutions in the country. To see highlights such as John Neumeier's 'Ballet Days' fans will literally camp out in front of the ticket office. Tickets are also available through the *Hamburg Tourism* hotline (see p. 123).

## BARS & CAFÉS

Unless otherwise stated, the city's trendy cafés are open every day from 10am or 11am. Most of them offer breakfast, and often brunch on Sundays. As a rule the bars and clubs only open up in the evenings. They close once the last people have left.

**DIE BANK** (132 C3) (*🗺 L6*)
Brasserie and bar located in an old bank – stunning interior and hotspot for the chic set. *Closed Sun | Hohe Bleichen 17 | tel. 040 2 38 00 30 | U 2 Gänsemarkt*

**THE CHUG CLUB** (144 A5) (*🗺 K7*)
Bartender Betty Kupsa and her team love mixing tequilas and offer *chugs*, or mini taster shots. Ask for the INSIDER TIP Chug menu with several taster cocktails – the last one is like a sweet dessert. *Daily from 6pm | Taubenstr. 13 | tel. 040 35 73 51 30 | U 3 St. Pauli*

**CIU** ☀ (133 E3) (*🗺 M6*)
In summer you're spoiled for choice between the chic bar indoors and the smart benches outside – if you sit outside you're more likely to be noticed and that's what it's all about – quite a wannabe crowd. *Daily from 4pm, Sun from 6pm | Ballindamm 14–15 | tel. 040 32 52 60 60 | S-/U-Bahn Jungfernstieg*

**GAZOLINE BAR** (143 D4) (*🗺 H6*)
The bar is long, the whiskies are good and the music is worth a listen: this is the best place to start or end your pub-crawl in Ottensen, especially when the bars around Alma-Wartenberg-Platz are getting overcrowded. *Daily (Sun from*

*3pm) | Bahrenfelder Str. 132 | tel. 040 3742 90 28 | bus and S-Bahn Altona*

## GOLEM (143 F5) (*ⓜ J7*)

This bar at the Fischmarkt attracts the in-crowd with its cocktails, old piano and the best jazz events in the city: **INSIDER TIP** *Fatjazz*, initiated by Hamburg saxophonist Gabriel Coburger *(Wed 8pm)*. If you prefer edgy, go a few doors further on to the live rock club *Hafenklang*. *Tue, Thu–Sun from 8pm (Fri–Sun from 10pm with admission) | Große Elbstr. 14 | bus 111 Fischauktionshalle*

## INSIDER TIP STRANDPAULI
(144 A5) (*ⓜ K7*)

There are a few beach clubs in Hamburg but this is the nicest, firmly established alongside the shipping piers. Don't miss the dance nights on the terrace. *Mid-March–Sept, in winter evening only, in the heated annexe | St Pauli Hafenstr. 89 | S-/U-Bahn Landungsbrücken*

## 20 UP LOUNGE & BAR ★ ⥼
(144 A5) (*ⓜ K7*)

Fabulous views: the bar overlooks Hamburg from the 20th floor of the *Empire Riverside Hotel*. The people of Hamburg love to show their guests this view of their city so the place is busy, and there is a dress code. *Daily from 6pm | Bernhard-Nocht-Str. 97 | tel. 040 3111 97 04 70 | S-/U-Bahn Landungsbrücken*

## CLUBS & DISCOS

## ANGIE'S NIGHTCLUB (144 A5) (*ⓜ K7*)

A neighbourhood perennial that has live music every evening – either from Angie's house band or invited guests. Good, danceable soul, funk and pop. *Fri/Sat from 10pm | 10 euros | Spielbudenplatz 27 | tel. 040 3177 88 11 | www.tivoli.de/gastro/angies | S 1, 3 Reeperbahn*

## CASCADAS (133 E3) (*ⓜ M6*)

The small streets in Hamburg City are hardly empty at night. Music fans gather on a corner near the Binnenalster lake: at *Cascadas*, you can listen to top-class concerts from Hamburg's jazz federation. If you're not a big fan of jazz, the bar also has other parties, e.g. Caribbean Nights and swing parties. *Ferdinandstr. 12 | S-/U-Bahn Hauptbahnhof*

## FRAU HEDI (144 A6) (*ⓜ K7*)

A different kind of harbour tour: in summer the **INSIDER TIP** party boat 'Frau Hedi' cruises around the harbour, and the passengers chill out and dance. *April–Oct Mon–Fri from 7pm, Sat/Sun from 6pm hourly, variable in winter |*

★ **Mojo Club**
The Mojo is back, so you can dance the night away → p. 84

★ **20 up Lounge & Bar**
Even the cool in-crowd gets excited by the breathtaking view! → p. 83

★ **Uebel & Gefährlich**
The scene is alive and well: dancing in an old bunker → p. 87

★ **Schmidt-Theater**
Cult status venue with glamour, show and song → p. 89

★ **Staatsoper Hamburg/Hamburg Ballet**
Two cultural treasures of the Hanseatic city → p. 88

★ **Thalia-Theater**
A class act: the finest theatre in town → p. 89

**MARCO POLO HIGHLIGHTS**

9–10 euros | Landungsbrücke 10/Innen-kante | www.frauhedi.de | S-/U-Bahn Landungsbrücken

### HAUS 73 (144 A3) (*ᗕ K5*)
Whether theatre, song-writer slams, po-litical debates or watching soccer, there's something going on every day. Frequent-ed by teenies and twenty-somethings at weekends; very popular with local bo-hemians during the week. The bar *Ga-lopper des Jahres* serves craft beer. *Dai-ly* | *Schulterblatt 73* | *tel. 040 43 09 39 75* | *www.dreiundsiebzig.de* | *metro bus 15 Schulterblatt*

### HOME OF BURLESQUE
The mixture of red-light area and feel-good bar organises erotic burlesque shows at different venues, where the la-dies show off their curves without shed-ding that final piece of clothing. *Dates and tickets see website: www.home-of-burlesque.com*

### KLUBHAUS ST PAULI (144 A5) (*ᗕ K7*)
Five floors of Kiez entertainment on the Reeperbahn: at ground level youngsters enjoy great dance music in the *Sommer-salon,* while older guests head for the *Schmidtchen,* the third stage owned by Tivoli boss Corny Littmann; on the first floor, things get crowded in the evenings at the *Kukuun* bar and disco, but then the kids, who had fun playing escape games and laser adventures, are already at home. *Spielbudenplatz 21–22* | *U 3 St Pauli*

### MOJO CLUB ★ (144 B5) (*ᗕ K7*)
The location beneath the 'Dancing Tow-ers' is unfortunately a bit too cool, but the music is simply amazing. *Several live concerts per week* | *prices and times vary* | *Reeperbahn 1* | *www.mojo.de* | *U 3 St Pauli*

# SPOTLIGHT ON SPORTS

Even reluctant sports fans will be cheered by the performance of Hamburg's latest top team: basketball players with Ham-burg Towers in Wilhelmsburg are already in the 2nd division. As well as their en-dearing image as underdogs, they al-ready have a cool group of cheerleaders and music-loving fans who beat drums and get the audience going *(hamburg towers.de)*. The city's soccer fans are used to some ups and downs. The dino-saur of the German Bundesliga HSV reg-ularly battles with relegation from the elite league, but the team's home stadi-um now has a fitting name: Volkspark-stadion *(hsv.de/en)*. The fate of FC St Pau-li is a roller-coaster ride and at Millerntor the team is either relegated to the 3rd division or wins promotion back to the 1st division. It hardly matters, as the fans stay loyal to their club like swans on the Alster lake. Season-ticket holders are en-vied but fans can easily watch the games at home. Just listening to the intro mu-sic as players walk onto the pitch – *Hells Bells* by AC/DC – gives you goose bumps from the Heiligengeistfeld. Hamburg's ex-sports heroes are on the up: the handball sports club enjoyed a meteor-ic rise, then went bankrupt. Since the 2016 season the new players won back the support of Hamburgers with their hard work and modest approach – and they were on a winning streak, although currently they are still in the 3rd division *(hamburg-handball.de)*.

Entertainment palace at Spielbudenplatz: Klubhaus St Pauli

## MS STUBNITZ (149 E1) *(Ⓜ N8)*

'MS Stubnitz' is anchored in the wild part of Hafencity where rusty old freight ships are moored. The storage area on this refrigerator shop (built 1964) was saved thanks to crowdfunding – there is a fantastic acoustic for theatre groups (experimental), parties (hip, often with plenty of electronica) and live gigs (all styles, but never mainstream). *Open for special programmes | Kirchenpauerkai 29 | ms.stubnitz.com | bus 111 Baakenhöft*

## NOCHTSPEICHER (144 A5) *(ⓂK7)*

Away from the turbulent side of the 'Kiez' is the 160-year-old warehouse with its first-class cultural programme, e. g. the best slam *Hamburg ist Slamburg*, bouncer readings, live concerts and the Dockside Swing parties. *Opening times depend on the programme | admission 6–22 euros | Bernhard-Nocht-Str. 69A | www.nochtspeicher.de | S 1, 3 Reeperbahn*

## OLIVIAS WILDE JUNGS

(144 A5) *(ⓂJ6)*

Germany's only male strip joint, for women only. Gogo boys and an hourly strip dance when the crowd goes wild – what more could a woman want? *Fri/Sat from 8pm, Nov-March from 9pm, closed Jan | admission 10 euros | Große Freiheit 32 | www.olivia-jones.de | S 1, 3 Reeperbahn*

### CINEMAS

## ABATON (144 C2) *(ⓂL5)*

Hamburg's nicest and one of the best art house cinemas in Europe. Afterwards you can discuss the movie in the **INSIDER TIP** *Abaton Bistro. Allende-Platz 3 | tel. 040 41320320 | www.abaton.de | metro bus 4, 5 Grindelhof*

## METROPOLIS (132 C3) *(ⓂL6)*

This cinema next to the opera house shows silent movies accompanied with live music. The place has been modernised but the artistic standards with great movie specials remain unchanged. *Kleine Theaterstr. 10 | tel. 040 342353 | www.metropoliskino.de | U 1 Stephansplatz*

## ZEISE KINOS (143 D4) *(ⓂH6)*

Good films (no blockbusters) are shown in the old propeller factory in Ottensen. *Friedensallee 9 | tel. 040 3908770 | www.zeise.de | metro bus 2 Friedensallee*

## PUBS & WINE BARS

### BORCHERS (136 C4) (𝄞 L2)
Borchers has been *the* pub in Eppendorf ever since 1906. Pleasant beer garden, Sept–April dance night every third Saturday in the month, Sunday brunch. *Daily | Geschwister-Scholl-Str. 1 | tel. 040 46 26 77 | metro bus 20, 22, 25 Eppendorfer Marktplatz*

### FC ST PAULI CLUBHEIM (144 B4) (𝄞 K6)
In the heart of the district is the St Pauli FC soccer stadium; the clubhouse is a public bar, with all the games shown live on a big screen. Beer garden open in the summer. *Mon–Fri from noon, Sat/Sun open for home games and Bundesliga highlights | Harald-Stender-Platz 1 | tel. 040 31 78 74 95 | U 3 St Pauli*

### FRAU MÖLLER (145 E4) (𝄞 N6)
The Lange Reihe in St Georg used to be one of the most colourful streets in Hamburg. Now it's been gentrified and only a few islands remain, including this pub (with good food and eight varieties of draught beer!). Local residents, actors from the nearby playhouse, hotel staff and of course visitors from out of town all gather here. *Daily | Lange Reihe 96 | tel. 040 25 32 88 17 | metro bus 6 Gurlittstraße*

### LANDHAUS WALTER (137 E4) (𝄞 N2)
A unique mixture: in the front, guests dine in the rustic restaurant with Hamburg's only real beer garden (in the park). At the back in the *Downtown Bluesclub* in the evenings the beat of the double bass makes the wine bottles shake! Blues concerts are fabulous and parties are popular with the over-40s generation. *Daily (Oct–March closed Mon) | Hindenburgstr. 2 | tel. 040 27 50 54 | www.eventcenter-hamburg.de | U 3 Borgweg*

### SAAL II (144 A3) (𝄞 K5)
The Saal bar is a lively, yet at the same time relaxed, venue near the *Rote Flora* and the busy bars of the Schanzenviertel on the piazza opposite. *Daily | Schulterblatt 83 | tel. 040 4 39 28 28 | S-/U-Bahn Sternschanze*

### INSIDER TIP ▶ ZUM SCHELLFISCHPOSTEN (143 F5) (𝄞 J7)
The old seaman's pub at the Fischmarkt has been enjoying a renaissance ever since a late-night TV show started being broadcast from here. *Daily | Carsten-Rehder-Str. 62 | tel. 040 38 34 22 | bus 111 Fischauktionshalle*

## LOW BUDGET

TV on Sunday and music on weekdays is free of charge at the *Pony Bar* **(144 C2)** *(𝄞 L5) (Allende-Platz 1 | www.ponybar.com | metro bus 4, 5 Grindelhof)*.

Their name says it all: the two guys who run the *Freundlich und Kompetent* **(146 A2)** *(𝄞 O4) (daily from 4pm | Hamburger Str. 13 | www.freundlichundkompetent.de | U 3 Mundsburg)* are just that: friendly and competent. They stage live music, sessions or slams – for free!

World-class opera and ballet performances **(132 C3)** *(𝄞 L6)* (see p. 88), and they're affordable, with tickets available from 10 euros.

Hamburg's churches are wonderful venues for affordable classical concerts, with or without choir. Info: *www.nordkirche.de/konzerte*

### FABRIK (143 D4) (🕮 H6)
Well-established venue in Altona; some bands have been performing here for decades. It doesn't have the best acoustics but the atmosphere makes up for that. Saturday night is often party night. *Barnerstr. 36 | tel. 040 39 10 70 | www.fabrik. de | bus and S-Bahn Altona*

### FREILICHTBÜHNE IM STADTPARK (138 A3) (🕮 O2)
Many local bands perform in the Stadtpark (city park), as well as really international acts such as Crosby, Stills & Nash. *Ticket hotline: 040 4 13 22 60 | kj.de/ event.html?id=42 | S 1 Alte Wöhr*

### KNUST (144 B4) (🕮 K6)
In the old abattoir, this club, which was once an infamous dive, has become an established concert venue and preferred haunt of St Pauli FC fans. *Neuer Kamp 30 | www.knusthamburg.de | U 3 Feldstraße*

### UEBEL & GEFÄHRLICH ★ (144 B4) (🕮 K6)
This venue has gained quite a reputation for its live music and party nights, which are very popular. The bands are pretty taken with the location – the 4th floor of a World War II bunker! The lift even has an attendant during performances. *Usually Wed–Sat from 8pm, parties from midnight | Feldstr. 66 | Medienbunker | www.uebelundgefaehrlich. com | U 3 Feldstraße*

# MUSICALS

The four biggest musical theatres belong to Stage Entertainment and run daily. At the *Mehr! Theater* the show runs change frequently. Stage tickets:

Film art in the factory hall: Zeise Kinos

tel. 01805 44 44 (*), online: www.stage-entertainment.de.

### THE LION KING (144 B6) (🕮 K7)
Disney's Lion King has long become a classic. The African tale dazzles with its amazing masks and costumes. A ferry will take you from the shipping piers to the opposite bank of the Elbe. *Theater im Hafen | Norderelbstraße 6 | S-/U-Bahn Landungsbrücken*

### MEHR! THEATER (133 F5) (🕮 N7)
Versatile building for simply 'more theatre': dance shows à la Dirty Dancing, concerts and orchestral performances. *Bankstr. 28/near Großmarkt | tel. 0180 5 20 01 (*) | www.mehr.de/en | metro bus 3 Lippeltstraße*

## OPERA & CLASSICAL MUSIC

### ELBPHILHARMONIE (132 C6) (ℳ L7)
If you like, you can spend your entire stay in Hamburg in the concert house enjoying music, artists' debates, kids' events and workshops (see p. 43) – that is, if you can get tickets. This was a real challenge when the venue first opened.

Musicals at the Theater im Hafen: The Lion King

Ticket tel. 040 35 76 66 66 | Platz der Deutschen Einheit 4 | bus 111 Kaiserkai/Elbphilharmonie

### STAATSOPER HAMBURG/ HAMBURG BALLETT ★
(132 C3) (ℳ L6)
John Neumeier's ballets are legendary; Kent Nagano took charge at the opera: both are a sure-fire guarantee of international flair on the Elbe. Dammtorstr. 28 | tel. 040 35 68 68 | www.staatsoper-hamburg.de/en | www.hamburgballett.de/en | U 1 Stephansplatz

### LAEISZHALLE (132 B3) (ℳ L6)
In 2018, the Laeiszhalle (a music and concert hall) is 110 years old. The Neo-Baroque style was once regarded as ultra-chic. Now, it's in the shadow of the Elbphilharmonie, but the symphonic orchestra directed by Jeffrey Tate still offers high-quality concerts. J.-Brahms-Platz 20 | tel. 040 35 76 66 66 | elbphilharmonie.de/en | metro bus 3 | bus 112 J.-Brahms-Platz

## SHOWS & CABARET

### INSIDER TIP ▶ NACHTASYL
(133 E4) (ℳ M6)
This bar on the top floor of the Thalia-Theater is used as an experimental stage for young talents. Witty pieces, readings, guest concerts and parties. Even when there is nothing going on, it is a nice place. Daily from 7pm | Alstertor 1 | tel. 040 32 81 44 44 | www.thalia-theater.de | S-/U-Bahn Jungfernstieg

### POLITTBÜRO (145 E4) (ℳ N6)
Biting left-wing satire in St Georg established by frontwoman Lisa Politt. Tickets 15 euros, reduced rate 10 euros | Steindamm 45 | tel. 040 28 05 54 67 | www.polittbuero.de | U 1 Lohmühlenstraße

## INSIDER TIP ▶ DAS SCHIFF
(132 C5) (*∅ L7*)

On board Europe's only seaworthy theatre ship, things get just as crowded as at the Fischmarkt when the audience throngs around the bar during the interval. Ideal for cabaret, comedy reviews and readings. *Tickets from 21 euros | Holzbrücke 2/Nikolaifleet | tel. 040 69 65 05 60 | www.theaterschiff.de | U 3 Rödingsmarkt*

## SCHMIDT-THEATER ⭐
(144 A5) (*∅ K7*)

The former president of St Pauli FC, Corny Littmann, is *the* Impresario on the Reeperbahn; his theatres *(Schmidt-Theater, Schmidts Tivoli)* enjoy cult status and stage a convincing blend of witty programmes and old favourites such as *Caveman* and *Die Königs vom Kiez. Spielbudenplatz 24 | tel. 040 31 77 88 99 | www.tivoli.de | S 1, 3 Reeperbahn*

## CASINO

### CASINO ESPLANADE (133 D2) (*∅ L6*)
Magnificent white building on the Esplanade: There are gaming machines in the hall *(daily from noon)*; in the casino itself the stakes are higher. *Daily from 3pm | admission 2 euros (ID required) | Stephansplatz 10 | tel. 040 3 34 73 30 | www.spielbank-hamburg.de/en | U 1 Stephansplatz*

## THEATRE

### DEUTSCHES SCHAUSPIELHAUS
(125 F3) (*∅ M6*)

Intendant Karin Beier heads the largest German dramatic art venue. The *Malersaal* hosts smaller plays, also for children and young people. *Kirchenallee 39–41 | tel. 040 24 87 13 | www.schauspielhaus. de/en | S-/U-Bahn Hauptbahnhof*

## KAMPNAGELFABRIK
(137 F5–6) (*∅ N3*)

Here we have dance and experimental theatre of the highest standard on the premises of an old engineering company. First-rate programme and fantastic summer festival in August. *Jarrestr. 20–24 | tel. 040 27 09 49 49 | www.kampnagel.de/en | bus 172, 173 Jarrestraße*

## OHNSORG-THEATER
(133 F3) (*∅ M6*)

This is only for those who can understand the Low German dialect – then you are in for a lot of down-to-earth fun. *Heidi-Kabel-Platz 1 | tel. 040 35 08 03 21 | www.ohnsorg.de | S-/U-Bahn Hauptbahnhof*

## ST PAULI THEATER
(144 A5) (*∅ K7*)

Neighbourhood theatre with a long tradition and varied programme. German TV stars often tread the boards. *Spielbudenplatz 29–30 | tel. 040 47 11 06 66 | www.st-pauli-theater.de | U 3 St Pauli*

## THALIA-THEATER ⭐
(133 E4) (*∅ M6*)

The finest theatre in town, with a very active director in Joachim Lux and several venues in the main building on Gerhart-Hauptmann-Platz and on Gaußstraße in Ottensen. *Alstertor 1 | tel. 040 32 81 44 44 | www.thalia-theater.de | S-/U-Bahn Jungfernstieg*

## WINTERHUDER FÄHRHAUS
(137 D4) (*∅ M2*)

This is far from superficial street theatre. In this successful privately owned theatre you can see funny and often satirical plays. Since 2017, Britta Duah is the first woman to direct the comedy theatre. *Hudtwalckerstraße 13 | tel. 040 48 06 80 80 | www.komoedie-hamburg. de | U 1 Hudtwalckerstraße*

# WHERE TO STAY

Hotel beds in Hamburg are plentiful. All major chains are represented in the city. Or perhaps you'd prefer a family-run hotel in one of the beautiful villas, or even a night on a ship? Be inspired!

There are more than 300 hotels and guest houses in Hamburg, and the number is on the rise. Luxury chains have also hit town. Whether at the top of the Elbphilharmonie, in Hafencity, the Speicherstadt or on the Außenalster – new, stylish hotels are opening everywhere. A wide selection of pleasant, often family-run hotels has also grown up over the years, plus hostels, B&Bs and guest houses. The city even boasts a few campsites. Events such as the anniversary of the port push the prices up quite a bit, as do trade fairs. The centrally located hotels are general-ly fully booked at such times – so book in advance. Cheap weekend rates and package deals are available through the *Hamburg Tourist Office (www.hamburg-travel.com)* as part of the 'Happy Hamburg' programme. Cheap combination deals are often available.

## HOTELS: EXPENSIVE

### ATLANTIC KEMPINSKI
(133 F2) (*m M6*)

Germany's last emperor once lived here – the oil painting in the lobby displays his portrait. Nowadays, Udo Lindenberg is a live-in guest – and his paintings also embellish one or another of the hotel walls. The wonderful garden terrace in the atrium courtyard is inviting if the weather is

A bunk, a luxury suite or a waterbed in a designer hotel – there's a variety of ways to spend the night in Hamburg

fine. *221 rooms | An der Alster 72–79 | tel. 040 28880 | kempinski.com/en/hamburg/hotel-atlantic | S-/U-Bahn Hauptbahnhof*

### EAST (144 A5) (🛍 K6)

Designer hotel in a converted steel foundry in St Pauli with beds (also waterbeds) in the middle of the room and bathrooms simply curtained off. Popular restaurant and bar. *128 rooms | Simon-von-Utrecht-Str. 31 | tel. 040 309930 | www.east-hamburg.de/en | U 3 St Pauli*

### FAIRMONT HOTEL VIER JAHRESZEITEN ★
(133 D3) (🛍 L6)

The Vier Jahreszeiten remains the best hotel in the city. The foyer is an oasis of tranquillity, especially beautiful at Christmas time when it's all decorated. Anyone unsure about how to behave here can always visit the 'etiquette course' (children too!). *156 rooms | Neuer Jungfernstieg 9–14 | tel. 040 34940 | www.fairmont-hvj.de | S-/U-Bahn Jungfernstieg*

Stay the night in an old water tower: Mövenpick Hotel

**GRAND ELYSÉE** (133 D1) (*🕮 L5*)
Hamburg's Steakhouse king, Eugen Block, has built a monument to himself with the *Grand Elysée*, which includes Hamburg's biggest ballroom. Non-residents are welcome to use the ● spa facilities. Hamburgers like to meet for an afternoon coffee in the lobby. *511 rooms | Rothenbaumchaussee 10 | tel. 040 41 41 20 | www.grand-elysee.com/en | S 21, 31 Dammtor*

**LOUIS C. JACOB** (141 E5) (*🕮 C–D6*)
Beautiful, privately owned hotel on the Elbchaussee with wonderful views of the Elbe. Lovingly designed down to the last oil painting above the fireplace. Any Blankenese local worth their salt will have got married here or at least celebrated a milestone birthday. On the terrace, immortalised by the artist Max Liebermann, you can eat divine cuisine under the lime trees. *85 rooms | double 258–315 euros, suites 385–998 euros | Elbchaussee 401–403 | tel. 040 82 25 50 | www.hotel-jacob.de | express bus 36 Sieberlingstraße*

**PRIVATHOTEL LINDTNER**
(150 C4) (*🕮 O*)
The Lindtner was always a good recommendation, even before anyone started talking about the 'leap across the Elbe'. Meanwhile, the Lindtner is also easy to reach by public transport; car drivers will find free parking spaces and a INSIDER TIP charging point for electric cars. *128 rooms | Heimfelder Str. 123 | tel. 040 79 00 90 | www.lindtner.com/en | bus 142 Heimfelder Straße*

**MÖVENPICK HOTEL HAMBURG**
(144 B3) (*🕮 K5*)
Spectacularly designed: spend the night within the thick walls of the second-tallest water tower in Europe and enjoy the view from the windows over the trade fair grounds. Its construction in the alternative Schanzenpark was bitterly contested. *226 rooms | Sternschanze 6 | tel. 040*

3 34 41 10 | www.moevenpick.com/en | S-/U-Bahn Sternschanze

### PARK HYATT (133 F4) (*ш M6*)
This hotel is famous for its comfortable beds, a fact also appreciated by the many famous names that have stayed the night in the converted *kontorhaus*. The peaceful lobby on the first floor with its view over the bustling Mönckeberg-straße is often used for business meetings. *252 rooms, 31 apartments | Bugenhagenstr. 8–10 | tel. 040 33 32 12 34 | www.hamburg.park.hyatt.com | S-/U-Bahn Hauptbahnhof*

### REICHSHOF HAMBURG
(133 F3) (*ш M6*)
The re-birth of a legend: in the old (new) Reichshof opposite the Hauptbahnhof Hamburgers meet once again in the heritage-protected restaurant *Slowmann* or for a drink in the leather armchairs of the *Bar 1910*. *278 rooms | Kirchenallee 34–36 | tel. 040 3 70 25 90 | www.reichshof-hotel-hamburg.de | S-/U-Bahn Hauptbahnhof*

### SIDE (132 C3) (*ш L6*)
Even the way to the WC is an object lesson for students of design. The theatre director Robert Wilson did the lighting in an interior dominated by wood and clean lines. In the *Meatery* restaurant: steaks at their best! *178 rooms | Drehbahn 49 | tel. 040 30 99 90 | www.side-hamburg.de/en/ | U 1 Stephansplatz*

## HOTELS: MODERATE

### HOTEL ALSTER-HOF
(133 D2) (*ш L6*)
Good news for pet owners – INSIDER TIP dogs are welcome here. The hotel is close to the Außenalster, a popular place for dog walkers. Nice rooms. *103 rooms |*

Esplanade 12 | tel. 040 35 00 70 | www.alster-hof.de | U 1 Stephansplatz

### AMERON HOTEL SPEICHERSTADT
(133 D6) (*ш L7*)
It's great to see how the old offices have been turned into smart rooms and the top floor into a spa. In the event of flooding, there's an emergency ladder down onto the car park next door, and the historic event room in the old coffee exchange is breathtakingly beautiful. *192 rooms | Am Sandtorkai 4 | tel. 040 6 38 58 99 31 | ameronhotels.com/en/hamburg-hotel-speicherstadt | metro bus 6, 111 Singapurstraße*

⭐ **The Westin Hamburg**
Sleep near the maestro – a unique hotel at the Elbphilharmonie → p. 94

⭐ **Baseler Hof**
Centrally located, friendly and steeped in tradition – a really beautiful hotel → p. 93

⭐ **Das kleine Schwarze**
Bed-and-breakfast in Eimsbüttel, with art and a retro-caravan in the garden → p. 99

⭐ **Henri**
Stylish living in a converted Kontorhaus office building → p. 99

⭐ **Fairmont Hotel Vier Jahreszeiten**
One of the world's finest hotels → p. 94

⭐ **Jugendherberge Auf dem Stintfang**
A hostel with the best (and cheapest) view → p. 94

**MARCO POLO HIGHLIGHTS**

**ASPRIA** (145 E1) (*N4*)

It can hardly get more chic than this: luxury sport club with pools, garden, saunas, equipment and wonderful fitness trainers, with really generously proportioned hotel rooms to boot. Everything's included, just like the well-heeled guests here on the Uhlenhorst. Try the special all-round tennis package with training sessions and massage. *48 rooms | Hofweg 40 | tel. 040 8 99 55 00 | www.aspria.com | metro bus 6 Averhoffstraße*

**BASELER HOF** ★ (133 D2) (*L6*)

Tradition meets warm hospitality in this centrally located hotel that belongs to the Association of Christian Hotels (VCH). The pleasant hotel restaurant, the *Kleinhuis*, has an acclaimed wine cellar. *172 rooms | Esplanade 11 | tel. 040 35 90 60 | www.baselerhof.de/index_en.php | U 1 Stephansplatz*

**EILENAU** (146 B2) (*O5*)

Hamburg's smallest 4-star hotel is idyllically situated on a canal at the edge of Ham-

# MORE THAN A GOOD NIGHT'S SLEEP

### Living at the Elbphilharmonie

How about a stay at Hamburg's new landmark? It's easy at the 🌿 ★ *The Westin Hamburg* (132 C6) (*L7*) (244 rooms | Platz der Deutschen Einheit 2 | tel. 040 8 00 01 00 | westinhamburg.com | bus 111 Kaiserkai/Elbphilharmonie | Expensive). The view from the curved windows on the upper levels is spectacular. Order a morning coffee from room service as the breakfast room is downstairs in the old store and only has arrow-slit windows.

### On the opposite shore

Another amazing view, but it's entirely different. From the *Hotel am Elbufer* (142 A6) (*E8*) (Focksweg 40a | tel. 040 7 42 19 10 | www.hotel-am-elbufer.de/ welcome | Budget) on the opposite side in Finkenwerder you're not overlooking the industrial areas but look upwards from the shore! The manager here still speaks 'Platt' German; there are only 15 rooms and the breakfast buffet is fabulous. In 20 minutes, the Hadag ferry No. 62 will take you to the landing stages.

### Hostels with de-luxe views

Youngsters always have a good deal. But now 'youth' hostels are also open for oldies. High above the landing stages is the 🌿 ★ *Jugendherberge Auf dem Stintfang* (132 A5) (*K7*) (357 beds | from 21.50 euros in dormitory | Alfred Wegener Weg 5 | tel. 040 31 34 88 | www.jugendherberge.de/en | S-/U-Bahn Landungsbrücken). A top location to enjoy fireworks at New Year – but it's best to stay indoors and avoid the thronging crowds.

### Now for an Alster view …

Artworks are in the rooms at 🌿 *Le Royal Méridien* (145 E3) (*N6*) (235 rooms | An der Alster 52–56 | tel. 040 2 10 00 | www.leroyalmeridienhamburg. com | Metrobus 6 Gurlittstraße | Expensive), and the views are of the Außenalster lake stretch as far as Harvestehude. The *Heritage* Restaurant is luxurious and has been stylishly renovated. Hotel guests can take the elegant glass lift that travels on the outer façade and offers sensational views.

burg-Uhlenhorst in two beautifully renovated art nouveau villas. It is privately run and all rooms are nicely appointed. Very small but really nice! *17 rooms | Eilenau 36–37 | tel. 040 2 36 01 30 | eilenau.gethamburg hotels.com/en | U 3 Uhlandstraße*

### GASTWERK HOTEL (143 D3) (*M G5*)
Made of lots of glass and brick, this building in the Otto-von-Bahren-Park in Bahrenfeld, a rather unattractive district, was among the first designer hotels in the city. An enormous gasworks once stood on the site; today there are flats, offices, a small lake and indeed hotels – a very interesting urban planning scheme. *141 rooms | Beim alten Gaswerk 3 | tel. 040 89 06 20 | www.gast werk.com/hotels-hamburg | metro bus 2, 3 Bornkampsweg*

### HOTEL HAFEN HAMBURG
(144 B5) (*M K7*)
Perched high above the Landungsbrücken: the rooms with views of the Elbe are more expensive. The view from the ● 〽 Tower Bar *(daily from 6pm | 12th floor)* however comes at no additional cost. Locals like to show off their city at this site. *380 rooms | Seewartenstr. 9 | tel. 040 31 11 30 | www.hotel-hamburg. de | S-/U-Bahn Landungsbrücken*

### HOTEL HEIMHUDE (144 C2) (*M L5*)
Friendly hotel with a regular clientele. Personal service is provided in a setting of restrained elegance. Rooms 17 and 18 even have balconies. *24 rooms | Heim huderstr. 16 | tel. 040 4 13 33 00 | www. hotel-heimhude.de/en | S 21, 31 Dammtor*

### LANDHAUS FLOTTBEK (141 F3) (*M E5*)
Country-house feeling in the lovely western part of Hamburg. Modernised thatched house with a delightful garden and gourmet restaurant. *25 rooms | Bar-*

Superior comfort: Le Royal Méridien

*on-Voght-Str. 179 | tel. 040 8 22 74 10 | www.landhaus-flottbek.de/en | express bus 37 Flottbeker Kirche*

### LINDNER PARK HOTEL HAGENBECK
(135 E4) (*M H2*)
Animal lovers will feel right at home among the wooden crocodiles and china elephants of this zoo themed hotel. Animal noises rather than music emanate from the hallway speakers, and a giant bronze bear welcomes guests at the entrance. A great place for the family and then of course there's Hagenbeck's Zoo just outside. *158 rooms | Hagenbeck str. 150 | tel. 040 8 00 80 81 00 | www. lindner.de/en | U 2 Hagenbecks Tierpark*

### NIPPON HOTEL (145 E1) (*M N4*)
Japanese lifestyle close to the Außenalster in Uhlenhorst, where clear, harmonious lines predominate. Guests walk

Quirky quarters: Das Feuerschiff

on tatami mats. *42 rooms | Hofweg 75 | tel. 040 2 27 11 40 | www.nipponhotel.de/ ?lang=en | metro bus 6 Zimmerstraße*

## SCANDIC ☀ ⊘ (132 B3) (*⑰ L6*)

Typical Scandinavia: bright, chic, sustainable, as well as child friendly. Wheelchair-accessible rooms. The 8th storey with larger rooms and suites and a separate breakfast buffet area is new – the view is also incredible! *325 rooms | Dammtorwall 19 | tel. 040 4 32 18 70 | www. scandichotels.com | U 2 Gänsemarkt*

## WEDINA (145 E4) (*⑰ N6*)

Hamburg's literature hotel is spread across five buildings in St Georg. Guests who book directly at the hotel are granted free admission to events in the nearby Literaturhaus. Many authors have stayed here and left autographed books behind. *61 rooms | Gurlittstr. 23 | tel. 040 2 80 89 00 | www.hotelwedina.de/en | metro bus 6 Gurlittstraße*

## 25H HAFENCITY (149 D1) (*⑰ M7–8*)

The rooms are called bunks, breakfast is served in the *Heimat-Hafen* (home port) restaurant, and in the Club Lounge on the 1st floor people laze around on soft cushions and listen to vinyl records. And all that in the middle of brand new Hafencity. *128 rooms | Überseeallee 5 | tel. 040 2 57 77 70 | www.25hours-hotels.com/en/hotels/ hamburg/hafencity | U 4 Überseequartier*

## HOTELS: BUDGET/HOSTELS

### HOTEL BAURS PARK (140 C4) (*⑰ B6*)

Right in the middle of the suburb Blankenese on the Elbe, five minutes from the market square and the pictorial Treppenviertel with its stairs and alleys. There are also family rooms for those with children. *24 rooms | Elbchaussee 573 | tel. 040 8 66 66 20 | www.baurspark.de | S 1, 11 Blankenese*

### CRISTOBAL HOTEL (137 E6) (*⑰ M3*)

Far from the madding crowd: this small, intimate hotel is situated near the Alster in lovely Winterhude. *18 rooms | Dorotheenstr. 52 | tel. 040 3 57 03 00 | www. hotel-cristobal.de/en | metro bus 6, 25 Gertigstraße*

### DAS FEUERSCHIFF (132 B6) (*⑰ L7*)

Bed down like an old sea dog in this red-painted former fire ship, in bunks that are small but comfortable. Listen to the Elbe lapping against the side of the wooden ship at night. INSIDER TIP Blue Monday jam sessions *(8.30pm)*, earplugs provided on the pillows. *7 rooms | Vorsetzen/ City Sporthafen | tel. 040 36 25 53 | www. das-feuerschiff.de | U 3 Baumwall*

### HOTEL HANSEATIN (132 B3) (*⑰ L6*)

A pretty, listed town house opposite the Laeiszhalle – for women only and with individually styled rooms. The reasonably priced breakfast (only 6.50 euros) will also make vegans happy. *13 rooms | Dragonerstall 11 | tel. 040 34 13 45 | www.hotel-hanseatin.de | metro bus 3 Johannes-Brahms-Platz*

### JUNGES HOTEL (145 E5) (*ω N6*)

Great for families: children love the fold-out bunks above their parents' bed, and the whole place is quite stylish, modern and congenial. The location is a little less attractive but it's only one stop on the U-Bahn to the *Hauptbahnhof* (main railway station). *127 rooms | Kurt-Schumacher-Allee 14 | tel. 040 4 19 2 30 | www.junges hotel.de/en | S-/U-Bahn Berliner Tor*

### HOTEL MICHAELIS HOF (132 B5) (*ω L7*)

This hotel in the Catholic Academy offers good value for money. Whether it's because of the cosy rooms or the other Christian guests, visitors automatically feel at home here. Only croissants and coffee for breakfast. *22 rooms | Herrengraben 4 | tel. 040 35 90 69 12 | www.michael ishof-hamburg.de/index_en.php | S 1, 3 Stadthausbrücke*

### MOTEL HAMBURG (136 B6) (*ω K3*)

Most importantly for drivers: there's somewhere to park your car. And that in Eimsbüttel is worth a lot. Thanks to its pristine 1950s style, the motel is now a listed building. *35 rooms | Hohe-luftchaussee 117–119 | tel. 040 4 20 41 41 | www.motel-hamburg.de | metro bus 5, 20, 25 Gärtnerstraße*

### MOTEL ONE (132 A4) (*ω K7*)

Despite its central location (the Reeperbahn can be seen from the upper floors) you'll get a good night's sleep as the rooms are soundproofed. The reception is open 24 hours a day; they'll even find you a dry place to park your bike. *437 rooms | Ludwig-Erhard-Straße 26 |*

tel. 040 35 71 89 00 | www.motel-one. com | U 3 St Pauli*

### HOTEL ST ANNEN (144 A4) (*ω K6*)

Charming, privately owned hotel with garden terrace garage – and a stone's throw from the vibrant Schanzenviertel and the Reeperbahn in the affluent part of St Pauli. *32 rooms | Annenstr. 5 | tel. 040 3 17 71 30 | www.hotelstannen. de | U 3 St Pauli*

### INSIDER TIP ▶ STADTHAUSHOTEL
(143 F4) (*ω J6*)

The façade may be uninviting but inside the atmosphere is all the more positive. A hostel managed by disabled people for disabled guests – and of course for others. *13 rooms | Holstenstr. 118 |*

*tel. 040 3 89 92 00 | www.stadthaus hotel.com | metro bus 15, 20, 25 Max-Brauer-Allee (Mitte)*

### STELLA MARIS (132 A5) (𝄞 K7)

This nice, modern hotel right at the port was once home to seamen, and today you can get modest, but well-kept double rooms. Internet terminals in the lobby. It's in the old Portuguese quarter and all around are nice little restaurants, mainly Portuguese and Spanish. *49 rooms | Reimarusstr. 12 | tel. 040 3 19 20 23 | www.stellamaris-hamburg.de/en | S-/U-Bahn Landungsbrücken*

### HOTEL VORBACH (144 C2) (𝄞 L5)

This is where guest lecturers at the university often live; occupying two nice old buildings on the Rothenbaum, the hotel is right at the campus. *116 rooms | Johnsallee 63–67 | tel. 040 44 18 20 | www.hotel-vorbach.de | U 1 Hallerstraße*

### WÄLDERHAUS ⊕ (149 E6) (𝄞 O)

This completely wooden house was built as part of the IBA, the International Building Exhibition, in Wilhelmsburg. Nature-lovers will be drawn to the well-presented in-house woodland exhibition. It also hosts numerous themed events on

Charming and trendy: the Superbude in St Pauli

### SUPERBUDE ST PAULI
(144 A3) (𝄞 K5)

Cool – cooler – ultra cool: this hostel is the second 'Superbude' in Hamburg, located on the edge of the trendy Schanzenviertel, at the border with St Pauli. Creative design in an old brick block. The website is a work of pop art. Everyone is very friendly; plenty of dormatories. *89 rooms | Juliusstr. 1 | tel. 040 8 07 915 8 20 | www.superbude.de/en | metro bus 3 Bernstorffstraße*

behalf of the German woodland protection organisation. *82 rooms | Am Inselpark 19 | tel. 040 30 21 56 100 | www.waelderhaus.de | S 3, 31 Wilhelmsburg*

### YOHO (144 A2) (𝄞 K5)

This small designer hotel in Eimsbüttel is housed in a city mansion dating from the turn of the 20th century. The old style has been cleverly combined with the modern. It's also affordable for young people: anyone under 26 gets a discount.

The Syrian restaurant *Mazza* serves superb food. *30 rooms | Moorkamp 5 | tel. 040 2 84 19 10 | www.yoho-hamburg.de/en | U 2 Christuskirche*

## CAMPING

**ELBECAMP** (150 B3) *(ﾉﾉ 0)*
This beach site on the banks of the Elbe at Blankenese seems almost surreal. Everything is simple but nice and indeed right on the Elbe. In summer it's quite idyllic, except for the occasional disturbance at night from barbecue parties next door. *April–Oct | tent from 7 euros, camper van from 15 euros | tel. 040 81 29 49 | www.elbecamp.de | express bus 48 Strandweg*

**KNAUS-CAMP** (150 C2) *(ﾉﾉ 0)*
This campsite next to Ikea in Schnelsen is not at all central, but it does offer a lot in the way of creature comforts. There are also static mobile homes. *Wunderbrunnen 2 | tel. 040 5 59 42 25 | www.knaus-camp.de/hamburg | A 7, exit Schnelsen-Nord, U 2 Niendorf Markt, then bus 191 Dornröschenweg*

## B & B/FLATS

**CLIPPER ELB-LODGE** (143 F5) *(ﾉﾉ J7)*
Ideal for temporary stays or longer (from 115 euros) – the boarding house is near the Fischmarkt at the Große Elbstraße. The apartments are beautifully equipped. Dogs are also welcome; also has a roof-terrace. *57 suites | Carsten-Rehder-Str. 71 | tel. 040 80 90 10 | www.clipper-boardinghouses.de | bus 111 Sandberg*

**HADLEY'S BED AND BREAKFAST** (144 B2) *(ﾉﾉ K4)*
Cosy rooms in an old building which was once a large hospital. Get your breakfast at *Hadley's* pub next door. **INSIDER TIP** There's often good jazz in the evenings there, too. *4 rooms, 1 family room | double rooms from 77 euros | Beim Schlump 85 | tel. 040 85 94 77 | www.b-bhadleys.de | metro bus 4, 15 Bundesstraße*

**HENRI** ★ (133 E4) *(ﾉﾉ M7)*
If Don Draper of 'Mad Men' really existed he would surely live here: stylish and sophisticated to the last detail, with glorious historic staircase and the beautifully designed *Henri-Bar*. You can have *abendbrod* (bread and savouries) in the open-plan bar/lounge area or get a ready meal to take up to your room's kitchenette. Double rooms 118–168 euros. *65 rooms | Bugenhagenstr. 21 | tel. 040 5 54 35 70 | www.henri-hotels.com | U 3 Mönckebergstraße*

**DAS KLEINE SCHWARZE** ★ (144 A1) *(ﾉﾉ J4)*
It's amazing what art lovers can do as guesthouse hosts. Black decor outside and with stylish interiors, this bed-and-breakfast gem is located in the heart of Eimsbüttel. The rooms are miniature galleries and the artworks regularly rotate. There is an old caravan in the garden – unbelievably cool way to spend the night. *From 114 euros. 8 rooms | Tornquiststr. 25 | tel. 040 23 93 99 11 | das-kleine-schwarze.com/en/hotel | metro bus 20, 25 Doormannsweg*

**OBERHOUSE APARTMENTS** (145 D1) *(ﾉﾉ L4)*
Beautifully done out apartments not only for business travelers: bright, friendly and nice for families, with kitchenette and fresh bread rolls. Well situated in Harvestehude, only 10 minutes' walk from the Außenalster. *32 apartments from 99 euros | Oberstr. 140 | tel. 040 41 33 39 00 | www.oberhouse.net/en/home | U 1 Klosterstern*

# DISCOVERY TOURS

## ① HAMBURG AT A GLANCE

| | | |
|---|---|---|
| **START:** ① Condi Lounge<br>**END:** ⑰ 20 up Lounge & Bar | | 1 day<br>Actual walking/<br>driving time<br>4 hours |
| **Distance:**<br>🚇 22 km/13.7 mi | | |

**COSTS:** 6 euros for the HVV 9am Day Ticket (or 11.20 euros for the 9am Group Ticket) plus food and drink

**IMPORTANT TIPS:** You can interrupt this tour at any time and carry on the next day, for example, if you wish to take a closer look at the individual sights.
① Condi Lounge open Mon–Fri from 8am, Sat/Sun from 10am

Would you like to explore the places that are unique to this city? Then the Discovery Tours are just the thing for you – they include terrific tips for stops worth making, breathtaking places to visit, selected restaurants and fun activities. It's even easier with the Touring App: download the tour with map and route to your smartphone using the QR Code on pages 2/3 or from the website address in the footer below – and you'll never get lost again even when you're offline.

TOURING APP

→ p. 2/3

Admittedly, this tour is quite a challenge and calls for a certain pace and stamina. But when you've completed it, you'll have earned the title of insider, even in the eyes of a genuine Hanseatic resident.

**08:00am** Start in classic Hanseatic style and enjoy a leisurely coffee in the ❶ Condi Lounge at the Hotel Vier Jahreszeiten. If you feel refreshed, you can set off. **Leaving the hotel, head right over the crossroads and turn left at Jungfernstieg! Opposite, you'll see the glimmer of the Alster lake. Carry on walking until you get to the Alsterfleet.** Now, your

❶ Condi Lounge

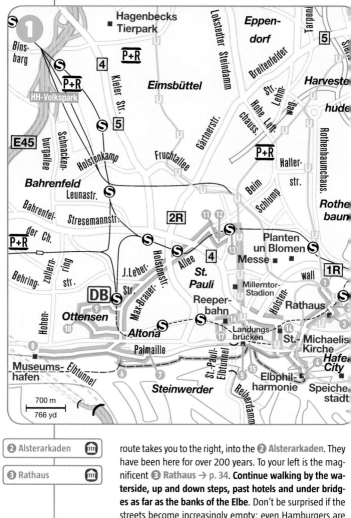

Hagenbecks
Tierpark

Eppen-
dorf

⑤

Bins-
barg

Lokstedter Steinkamp

Tarpen

HH-Volkspark

P+R

④

Kieler Str.

Eimsbüttel

Harveste

Breitenfelder

Str.-Lehm-weg

hude

Hohe Luft chauss.

E45

Schnaacken-burgallee

⑤

Holstenkamp

Gärtnerstr.

Fruchtallee

P+R

Haller-

Rothenbaumchauss.

Bahrenfeld

Leunastr.

Beim

str.

Rothe

Bahrenfel-

Stresemannstr.

Schlump

baun

der Ch.

2R

⑪⑫

P+R

Behring-

zollern-

ring

str.

J.Leber-

Holstenstr.

Allee

④

⑬

Planten
un Blomen

Messe ▪ ▪

1R

DB

Str.-

Max-Brauer-

St.
Pauli

Millerntor-
Stadion

Reeper-
bahn

wall

Holsten-

①

Rathaus

Ottensen

⑨

⑩

Altona

⑯

⑰ Landungs-
brücken

⑭

③

Hohen-

⑧

Palmaille

St.-Pauli-
Elbtunnel

⑮

St.- Michaelis
Kirche

Museums-
hafen

Elbtunnel

⑥

⑦

Steinwerder

Reiherdamm

Elbphil-
harmonie

Elbe

Hafen
City

Speiche-
stadt

700 m
766 yd

---

② Alsterarkaden 🏛

③ Rathaus 🏛

route takes you to the right, into the ② **Alsterarkaden**. They have been here for over 200 years. To your left is the magnificent ③ **Rathaus** → p. 34. **Continue walking by the waterside, up and down steps, past hotels and under bridges as far as the banks of the Elbe.** Don't be surprised if the streets become increasingly empty; even Hamburgers are often unfamiliar with this section of the 'Alsterwanderweg'. If you are reasonably fit and enjoy walking, this will take you roughly 20 minutes.

**11:00am** Building work has been ongoing for years at the Schaartorschleuse (lock). Perhaps, they've finally finished and you arrive at the banks of the River Elbe under the bridges – otherwise, take the top road, which isn't much further. **Go briefly to the right, then left across the Niederbaumbrücke.** The small brick building is familiar to German TV viewers as the police station in the ZDF series *Notruf Hafenkante*. **Remain on the path running along the Sandtorkai, then take the first turn right across the drawbridge till you reach the foot of the ❹ Elbphilharmonie → p. 43.** No queues at the 'Elphi'? Then seize the opportunity and go to the plaza square, admire the view and descend again. If you're organized, you will have booked a timed ticket in advance. Back on the lower level, board the No. 72 Hadag ferry at the **'Elbphilharmonie' landing stage.** You should purchase an HVV-day ticket (it's also valid on the U- and S-Bahn), and enjoy the short ferry ride for 10 minutes to the ❺ Landungsbrücken → p. 38. **Change boats here and take No. 62 towards Finkenwerder.** You pass by the **Fischmarkt → p. 50**, the **Große Elbstraße → p. 50**; to the left are the docks of the Blohm + Voss shipyard.

**12:30pm** Get off at the ❻ Dockland → p. 50 landingstage. If you're fit enough, climb the steps up to the **INSIDER TIP** roof of the futuristic office building – diagonally opposite are the halls of the Fischmarkt, where fish is traded till the early hours of the morning. Has the smell of fish whet your appetite? Then it's off to the upmarket snack bar ❼ **Hummer Pedersen → p. 73.** **To get there, turn right along Van-der-Smissen-Straße, past the cruise centre, round the bend and then off a little to the right into Große Elbstraße** – the attractive glass façade of the fish dealer's, which also sells lunches, is visible from afar. Suitably refreshed, you return on foot, that is, **back downstream along the Elbe for approx. 30 minutes** as far as the old captains' houses at ❽ Övelgönne → p. 51. Stop for a quick coffee on one of the museum ships at the **Museumshafen, then take bus No. 112 and travel to Altona station.**

**03:00pm** Since it's still only early afternoon, there is time for a stroll through the pleasant streets of ❾ Ottensen → p. 51 with its shops, restaurants, pubs and alternative businesses. **Leave the station via the Ottenser Hauptstraße,** then you are right in the thick of things. Alternative lifestyle meets everyday Turkish, combined with the chic creative scene of the advertising agencies, architects' offices and media companies now populating the converted industrial properties here. **Continue along Ottensener Hauptstraße to the end. When you reach the square named Bei der Reitbahn, go**

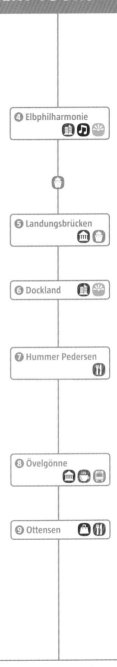

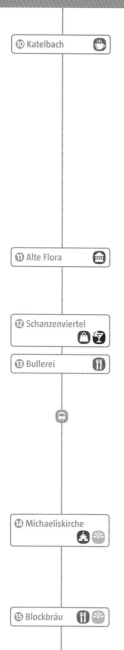

**to the left into Große Brunnenstraße.** At the next junction you'll come across the legendary coffee house ⑩ **Katelbach** *(daily from noon | Große Brunnenstr. 60)* where they roast the beans on the premises. Treat yourself to a cappuccino. Then continue your way: **out of the door and left, at the next crossroads head left into Keplerstraße and go right to the end. Over the crossroads turn sharp right into Rothestraße, until the end.** Pay attention as all the streets look similar – that's typical for Ottensen where old and new, chic and shabby buildings stand close together. **Where Rothestraße meets the Holländische Reihe, take the No. 15 bus (Rothestraße stop) in the direction of Alsterchaussee:** you can enjoy a rest now for a good 15 minutes.

`04:00pm` **Get out at the Schulterblatt station, backtrack and then turn left into the road of the same name.** Pass under the railway line and ahead of you a little to the right stands Hamburg's most controversial building, the ⑪ **Alte Flora**. Formerly a theatre, this run-down structure has been a squat for years now and a symbol of the fight against gentrification. There are regular street riots here every 1 May. **You continue down Schulterblatt** and find yourself in the middle of the trendy ⑫ **Schanzenviertel**: pubs, shops, lots of tourists. **Stay on Schulterblatt for a while, then turn left into Susannenstraße and at the end turn left again into Schanzenstraße.** Tim Mälzer's restaurant ⑬ **Bullerei** → p. 67 is opposite. In summer, you can grab a burger outside at the bar. Carry on, **again under the railway line, to the right.** You now come to the S-Bahn station and behind it the station for the **U3. Take this in the direction of Barmbek and travel the two stops to St Pauli.**

`06:00pm` **Leave the U-Bahn (at the Millerntorplatz exit) and cross the road at the traffic lights.** To the right is the temptation of the Reeperbahn, but it's time for culture first: **walk along the right-hand side of the road past the park to Ludwig-Erhard-Straße.** There is an ugly office block in front of you and directly behind it the tower of the ⑭ **Michaeliskirche** → p. 39. **Turn right onto the Englische Planke** and you find yourself almost in front of the beautiful church. There's enough time to take a guided tour and climb the tower (the church closes at 8pm, in winter at 6pm). **Leaving the Michel, turn left towards the Elbe. Walk along the river bank to the right as far as the Landungsbrücken and into the** ⑮ **Blockbräu**: first-class steaks and light beer brewed on the premises. The view from the terrace is magnificent!

**⑩ Katelbach**

**⑪ Alte Flora**

**⑫ Schanzenviertel**

**⑬ Bullerei**

**⑭ Michaeliskirche**

**⑮ Blockbräu**

`08:00pm` Now it's time for a little nightlife, and it's just one U-Bahn station away: *U3,* **back again to St Pauli station, but this time go in the other direction to the** ⑯ **Reeperbahn** → p. 40. There's not much left to say about this street. There is certainly no shortage of watering holes of various kinds. A great place for a drink is the ⑰ **20 up Lounge & Bar** → p. 83 on the 20th floor of the **Empire Riverside Hotel** at the end of Davidstraße/corner of Bernhard-Nocht-Straße. Fantastic view of the port at night!

⑯ Reeperbahn

⑰ 20 up Lounge & Bar

## ② UP AND DOWN THE STEPS OF BLANKENESE

| START: ❶ Blankenese S-Bahn station | 4 hours |
|---|---|
| END: ❾ Süllberg | Actual walking time |
| | 1 hour |

| Distance: | easy |
|---|---|
| 🔁 2.5 km/1.5 mi | 📊 Height: 75 m/246.1 ft |

**COSTS:** Approx. 20 euros/person for coffee and a snack, possibly a bus ticket (Warning: supplement for express bus!)
**WHAT TO PACK:** Fitness for climbing up and down the steps!

**IMPORTANT TIPS:** The 'Mountain Goat' (bus No. 48) runs from the destination at ❾ **Süllberg** back to Blankenese S-Bahn station.

What, mountain climbing in Hamburg? But of course! In Blankenese, a district directly on the Elbe! Put on your hiking boots and clamber up through the 'Positano of the North' – accompanied all the way by superb views of the river.

`12:00pm` **The starting point in** ⭐ **Blankenese is at** ❶ **Blankenese S-Bahn station**. An initial warm-up is provided by the short climb to the ❷ **Gossler-Haus**. **At the traffic lights, head diagonally right along Blankeneser Landstraße; on the right from the narrow pavement you'll now notice, or a little later, several steps leading up to Gossler Park.** Can you see an impressive white manor house slightly higher up? It was used as a government office over many years; today it is the conference centre of a private university. **Now the route goes downhill and across the traffic lights on Blankeneser Landstraße into Kirschtenstraße.** The first refreshments await: scones in ❸ **Lühmanns Teestube** *(daily | Blankeneser Landstr. 29 | tel. 040 86 34 42)*. **Continue along Kirschtenstraße, with the stately, old grammar school on the left, over the zebra crossing and then left**

❶ Blankenese S-Bahn station

❷ Gossler-Haus

❸ Lühmanns Teestube

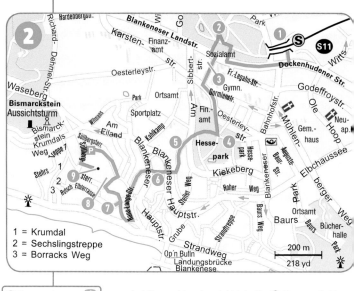

1 = Krumdal
2 = Sechslingstreppe
3 = Borracks Weg

**4 Hessepark**

and at the next turning right into the **4 Hessepark**. The **Hessehaus** is now a school run by the Evangelical Church.

**01:00pm** Walk down across the grass and by the circle of benches take the path to the right and leave the park. Follow the road called Kiekeberg briefly to the left, then turn right onto the **5 Charitas Bischoff Steps**. Voilà – the descent begins, in the heart of the 'Treppenviertel' ('staircase quarter'). The old houses stand within arm's reach to the left and right, separated only by steep steps and narrow pathways. You can peep into gardens and through kitchen windows; up to the right are the flags on the Süllberg; below you, the glistening Elbe. Carry on downhill, **crossing Blankeneser Hauptstraße**. Perhaps the 'Mountain Goat' minibus will just be passing, and you could take a ride with it down to the banks of the Elbe. The footpath down via the **6 Schlagemihls Steps** is prettier. **Cross the main road again. Pass by No. 38 opposite and turn left into Hans-Lange-Straße.** You're almost at the Elbe.

**02:00pm** But you came here to climb, of course, so it's on upwards again: **just where the last cars are parked go right, up the Elbterrasse a short way.** Notice the historic **7 Dreehuhs** houses built for three fishermen's families (Nos. 4–6), then head up to the right on the Süllbergter-

**5 Charitas Bischoff Steps**

**6 Schlagemihls Steps**

**7 Dreehuhs**

Blankenese's Treppenviertel has its own special charm – final ascent to the Süllberg

rasse. Watch out, it gets steep here. **At the top go left and then right** to arrive at ⑧ **Kaffeegarten Schuldt** *(in summer daily, in winter Fri–Sun only | tel. 040 86 24 11 | www.kaffeegarten-schuldt.de),* run by the same family for over 130 years now. The cake is home-made, the atmosphere unique. Now you've almost made it. **Go left out of the café and downhill for 200 m/656 ft, then take the next path up to the left.** After a few steps you'll arrive at the final ascent to the ⑨ **Süllberg**, a luxury restaurant → p. 66, hotel and beer garden. From here you have an amazing view over the Elbe and can enjoy a cool beer – what bliss!

⑧ Kaffeegarten Schuldt

⑨ Süllberg

---

**3**

# CYCLE TOUR THROUGH HAFENCITY

| | |
|---|---|
| **START:** ① Unileverhaus<br>**END:** ⑬ Magellan-Terrassen | **3 hours**<br>Actual cycling time<br>40 minutes |
| Distance:<br>➡ 5 km/3.1 mi | |

**COSTS:** approx. 12.50 euros for bike rental; you can even park your city bike en route, e. g. at the station near the U4 at the Hafencity University, and rent one again later, thus saving rental charges.

**IMPORTANT TIPS:** Hafencity is set to be a giant building site for decades to come; changes to traffic routes are possible.

The tour takes you through Hafencity, across bridges and along brand-new roads, past building sites and museums and includes a detour into the Speicherstadt. Discover a district pushing relentlessly eastwards, between gleaming office blocks, boulevards and a life at street level which is just getting off the ground.

❶ Unileverhaus

❷ Überseequartier

❸ Störtebeker-Denkmal

❹ Magdeburger Hafen

❺ Hafencity University

❻ View Point Hafencity

❼ Ökumenisches Forum

**11:00am** The starting point is the Stadtrad (city bike) depot at the Strandkai in front of the ❶ Unileverhaus → p. 46. Here is the new Grasbrookpark, **INSIDER TIP** a super playground with a fitness trail for grown-ups. Diagonally opposite are the brightly coloured containers of the temporary cruise ship terminal. You might see a luxury liner such as the 'Aida' at anchor. **Pass the terminal on your right and cycle around the left-hand bend past the new U4 station to the heating plant then turn right into the Überseeallee.** On the left is the ❷ Überseequartier the district's shopping area. **Turn left just before the Magdeburger Brücke and via the Osakaallee come to the** ❸ Störtebeker-Denkmal **down in front of the Busanbrücke.** Opposite is the magnificent warehouse building housing the maritime museum → p. 44.

**Cycle over the bridge,** and you come to the ❹ Magdeburger Hafen with the large-scale Elbarkaden. You can leave the bike below and enjoy a stroll on the upper level for several minutes. In summer, there are pleasant bars, in winter it's cold and empty here. At the end of the arcades on the left is the headquarters of Greenpeace. The exhibition in the foyer can be viewed free of charge *(Mon–Fri 9am–5pm, April–Oct, incl. Sun)*. Continue cycling further down the promenade, always keeping the lake on your right. Head under the bridge towards the angular building of the ❺ Hafencity University: This is where future urban planners and architects study. The Unicafé has a terrace affording a premium view of the Baakenhafen. **Cycle round the building and right onto the new Baakenhafenbrücke,** at the end of which is the ❻ View point Hafencity → p. 47. Ahead of you is the new district: Baakenhafen. The first houses are finished and soon several hundred people will live here.

**12:00pm** Turn back and cycle the short distance to Shanghaiallee where you turn right. To your left, you'll see a building with a curved façade and right at the top is a church bell: the small chapel belongs to the ❼ Ökumenisches Forum and is an oasis of calm. Take a short break and enjoy a fair-trade coffee in the Weltcafé ❿ Elbfaire → p. 70. Diagonally opposite the Forum is the automobile museum Prototyp → p. 46. **You then cycle in front of the**

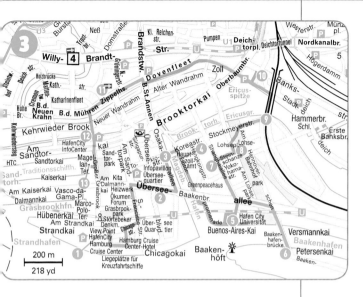

museum into the tiny Steinschanze and Steinstraße and end up directly in **⑧ Lohsepark** → p. 44. Many residents find the green lung too small, but it's better than nothing. The park is also a memorial. It was once the location of Hanover railway station. It was from here between 1940 and 1945 that deportation transports left for the death camps. A simple plaque commemorates this. Until the documentation centre is completed, a temporary pavilion tells the story of those dark days. **Keep left, leave the park and continue cycling to the right down Stockmeyerstraße.** On the other side of the canal you can see the reflective façade of Germany's news hub: its famous current-affairs magazine, *Der Spiegel*, has its magnificent headquarters here. **Continue along Stockmeyerstraße as far as the railway bridge.** There, right under the tracks, is an odd, lopsided brick house. This is the **⑨ Oberhafen-Kantine** → p. 71, once a snack bar for dockworkers and now a restaurant, in which you can treat yourself to get your strength up again. Immediately behind lies the Oberhafen-Quartier, home to representatives of the creative industry.

**01:00pm After the snack bar, continue across Oberhafen bridge (rail traffic travels overhead) and head left to flood protection barrier that you can cycle along.** Voilà: you've arrived at the **⑩ Deichtorhallen** → p. 42, today used as an ex-

hibition centre. **Cross the main road and continue along the flood protection barrier at the rear of the Deichtorcenter. Keep to the waterside along the edge of the Zollkanal and cycle parallel to the Speicherstadt.** After about 300 m/984 ft you'll pass the beautiful ⑪ **Katharinenkirche** (Church of St Katherine). Some 100 m/328 ft further on, the double-decker Kibbelstegbrücke spans the canal. Pedestrians walk on the upper level, **cyclists take the ramp down** and cruise into the ⑫ **Speicherstadt** → p. 41, a brick ensemble dating back to the Wilhelmine era. **The second part of the bridge takes you across to Große Grasbrook**, where after 100 m/328 ft you will arrive at the ⑬ **Magellan-Terrassen**. The old Elbphilharmonie Pavillon is still here, although the main building was finished some time ago. Return your bikes to the depot at the corner of the Kaiserkai and glance back at Hamburg's new landmark, the Elbphilharmonie.

⑪ Katharinenkirche

⑫ Speicherstadt

⑬ Magellan-Terrassen

# ④ ONCE AROUND THE AUSSENALSTER

| START: ❶ Hotel Atlantic END: ⑪ Hotel Vier Jahreszeiten | 6 hours Actual walking time 2 hours |
|---|---|
| Distance: ➡ 7.5 km/4.7 mi | |

COSTS: approx. 20 euros/person for coffee and a snack, boat rental 12 euros

IMPORTANT TIPS: Here, on fine summer days, and at weekends in particular, half of Hamburg is up and about. If you'd prefer things a little quieter, you should do the tour in the week or start early. Visit to the ❻ Imam Ali Mosque by appointment only

The circular footpath will show you many sides of Hamburg: sport and culture, civic pride and patronage. The path around the Außenalster is 7.5 km/4.7 mi long, ideal for a jog – which is what countless locals do every day.

❶ Hotel Atlantic

**10:00am** A lovely place to start your tour around the ★ *Außenalster* is the dazzlingly white ❶ **Hotel Atlantic** → p. 90, which was built in 1909. At that time, the cruise industry was experiencing its first boom, and it was at the Atlantic that the wealthy passengers waited to board their ships. **Cross over the road to the Alster shore and turn**

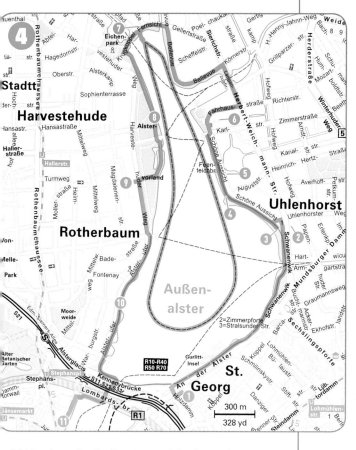

right. **Passing various landing stages and the Pieper Sailing School → p. 125, take a stroll along the southeast bank**. At Schwanenwik 38 is the ❷ **Literaturhaus** *(www.literaturhaus-hamburg.de),* a place where you could spend the whole day: with a ballroom decorated with stucco, a restaurant, café, bookshop and readings. But you're here for the fresh air after all, so now return to the Alster shore and take a few steps along as far as the trendy ❸ **Alsterperle** *(daily),* where you can stop for a break. Housed in a converted public toilet, the snack bar is tiny, but enjoys cult status because it's a wonderful place to relax over a bowl of pea soup or with a refreshing beer and enjoy the view across the Alster at the same time.

❷ Literaturhaus

❸ Alsterperle

Collective relaxation at the Alsterperle

**11:30am** The walk continues along the Schöne Aussicht. The name says it all, as it means 'beautiful view' in German. Indeed, the view back to the city gets progressively more beautiful! You could take another break at this point. The ❹ **Café Hansasteg** *(in summer daily, in winter Sat/Sun only | Schöne Aussicht 20a | www.cafehansasteg.de)* gives you the feeling you could be on Lake Como: a low hedge, old-fashioned lamps, tables directly by the water. Don't be alarmed if you see a lot of policemen in front of house No. 26 on the right. They'll be there for security reasons. Built by Martin Haller in 1868, this Alster villa is the official ❺ **guest house of the Senate**, the city parliament. The first visitor to stay here after the war was the Queen, later to be followed by Charles and Diana. A little further on stands a completely different kind of building: the ❻ **Imam Ali Mosque** *(en.izhamburg.com)*. Built in 1961, it is now an important centre for Hamburg's Shia Muslim community. Visitors are welcome, but must apply in advance. Directly opposite we return to good old Hanseatic values: the NRV, Hamburg's most traditional sailing club, is based here. You can't get lost at this point, even though the road now veers briefly away from the Alster. **Turn left into Herbert-Weichmann-Straße and beyond the bridge left again into Bellevue,** with its string of magnificent villas. At the top end of the Alster, at the Krugkoppelbrücke, is ❼ **Bobby Reich → p. 67** and its popular outdoor bistro. **INSIDER TIP** Rent a canoe or rowing boat and head out onto the water for an hour – after which you will certainly have earned a rest on the delightful waterside terrace.

**02:00pm** Continue walking along the green banks of the western shore. The ❽ **Alsterpark** has only been accessible to the public since 1953. Prior to that the land belonged to the private villas along Harvestehuder Weg. It gets packed here on sunny weekends, making it difficult to lay claim to one of the fine wooden chairs. Publishers of iconic German poet Heinrich Heine, Hoffmann und Campe, still reside in No. 42. Fancy a quick detour? **Turn right behind the** *Cliff-Alsterkaffee,* **cross Harvestehuder Weg and walk up Milchstraße.** Now you are in ❾ **Pöseldorf**, where designer Jil

❹ Café Hansasteg

❺ Guest house
of the Senate

❻ Imam Ali Mosque

❼ Bobby Reich

❽ Alsterpark

❾ Pöseldorf

Sander began her career. There are several art galleries, chic shops, cafés and restaurants. No. 12 Milchstraße, the former **Budge Palais**, is now home to the city's music academy.

**03:30pm** You're almost at the end of your walk. Is the sun shining? Pause at the banks of the ⑩ **Alster lake** in front of the former US consulate building (the 'white house') by the waterside and head for one of the picturesque benches placed here. It's a beautiful spot and opposite is the Hotel Atlantic where you started your circular tour. Now head back to the city. Continue along the shore, passing a number of rowing clubs, a restaurant and a sailing club as you approach the Kennedybrücke. **At this point, use the pedestrian tunnel under the Kennedy and Lombard bridges to take you directly onto the Neuer Jungfernstieg.** The walk ends the way it began: in a luxury hotel. Treat yourself to a drink in the bar of the ⑪ **Hotel Vier Jahreszeiten** → p. 91!

⑩ Alster lake

⑪ Hotel Vier Jahreszeiten

# ⑤ WITH THE 'WILDE 13' THROUGH WILHELMSBURG

| START: | ❶ Veddel S-Bahn station | **6 hours** |
| END: | ❶ Veddel S-Bahn station | Actual travel time approx. 1.5 hours |

Distance:
⬄ 15 km/9.3 mi

COSTS: Single ticket 2.20 euros, HVV 9am Day Ticket 6.20 euros

IMPORTANT TIPS: If you have bought a HVV Day Ticket, you can hop on and hop off the bus as often as you like. The buses on route M13 operate in the daytime every 4 to 6 minutes. ❺ **Energiebunker** open only Fri noon–6pm and Sat/Sun 10am–6pm

The 'Wilde 13' is the name given by the Wilhelmsburger to bus route M13, which scuttles across the Elbe island. Island? Yes, the district is one of the largest populated river islands in Europe. It has high-rise blocks next to farms, stacks of container next to arts centres, Turkish snack bars and traditional German restaurants, architects' houses from the International Building Exhibition and a sports park.

**10:00am** The starting point is ❶ **Veddel S-Bahn station**. **Several No. 13 buses are already waiting on the square in front of the station.** Vehicles roll in all the time, and away you go, **under the railway bridge and straight ahead.** Get out at the second stop, **Harburger Chaussee**, interrupting

❶ Veddel S-Bahn station

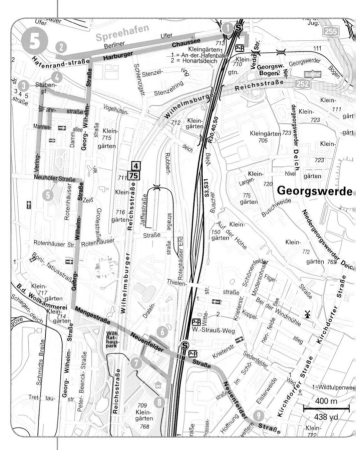

**❷ Spreehafen** 🚶 ❀

your journey for the first time. To the right behind the green dyke is the **❷ Spreehafen**. It was 2013 before the customs fence was taken down here; this was previously a free port area and off limits. Now, pedestrians can stroll along the inside of the dyke on the 'Alster of the South'. Back at the bus station you notice the contrast between the romance of the water and the dismal high-rise flats and commercial premises on the other side of the road. They bear witness to the fact that Wilhelmsburg was for a long time a neglected district and, in part, still is.

**Continue with the next 'Wild No. 13'. Immediately, the driver steers you into the Reiherstiegviertel, a colourful**

district featuring Gründerzeit houses and multicultural vibes. Get off at the ❸ Stübenplatz. There's a twice-weekly market here on Wednesdays and Saturdays (until 1pm). Have a milky Portuguese coffee, a *galão*, at ❹ O Seu *(daily | Veringstr. 26)* to get your strength up, **then continue on foot 15 minutes down Veringstraße as far as Neuhöfer Straße. Turn left down here;** ahead of you is the giant ❺ INSIDER TIP ▶ Energiebunker. Its conversion from an air-raid bunker to a source of renewable energy formed part of the IBA International Building Exhibition (2006–13) in Wilhelmsburg. Inside there's bags of information on the IBA. Some 30 m/98.4 ft up is Café Vju (pronounced 'view'), which also offers a sensational one across the Elbe and Hamburg. **Leaving the bunker, turn left back to the Veringstraße stop.**

Hamburg's environmental authority

`12:00pm` The bus passes the Rathaus (not worth getting out for), which stands like an isolated fortress at the bridge over the dual carriageway. Get off at the **Inselpark** stop. Here (opposite on Neuenfelder Straße) is Hamburg's colourful and futuristic ❻ Environmental Authority *(www.hamburg.de/bsu)*. Inside, there is a model of the city and you can find out about urban development in Hamburg. Back outside again, take a look across the street at the ❼ IBA architects' houses. Behind these is the ❽ Inselpark Wilhelmsburg, venue for the International Garden Show (IGS) in 2013. It's now a great place to spend a few hours – at the playground, in the skater park or simply going for a stroll.

`03:30pm` Get back on the 'Wilde 13' at *Inselpark.* Highrise blocks and traffic dominate the centre of Wilhelmsburg around the S-Bahn station. You make rapid progress, and suddenly a huge field pops into view ahead of you on the left. This is where the rural part of the island begins, criss-crossed by drainage canals. A high-rise residental estate, ❾ Kirchdorf, sprang up in this idyll in the 1970s – it's no beauty, but is populated meanwhile by a very vibrant community. Your journey ends here; **the bus which brings you back to ❶ Veddel S-Bahn station is already waiting for you on the other side (25 minutes).**

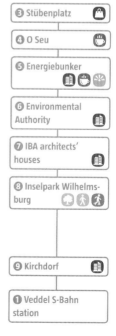

❸ Stübenplatz 🛍️

❹ O Seu ☕

❺ Energiebunker 🏛️ ☕ ❋

❻ Environmental Authority 🏛️

❼ IBA architects' houses 🏛️

❽ Inselpark Wilhelmsburg 🌳 🚶 🏃

❾ Kirchdorf 🏛️

❶ Veddel S-Bahn station

# TRAVEL WITH KIDS

There are big ships in the harbour and little paddleboats on the Alster, sand for building castles along the Elbe and many museums that have children's programmes. Even more, there are family friendly musicals like 'Lion King' and Germany's oldest theater for children. What more could a family want?

### CHILDREN'S THEATRE/ALLEETHEATER
(143 E4) (*H6*)

Children are taken seriously here – since 1968. In the evening there are operas for grown-ups. Tickets from 16 euros, performances usually on Fri, Sat and Sun. *Max-Brauer-Allee 76 | tel. 040 38 25 38 | kindertheater.alleetheater.de | metro bus 15, 20, 25 Gerichtsstraße*

### HAGENBECKS TIERPARK ★
(135 E4) (*H2*)

One of Europe's biggest tropical aquariums with Madagascan lemurs roaming free, a sensational orang-utan house, elephants that can be hand fed as well as an icy lake that is safe to walk on with INSIDER TIP walruses (the only ones in Germany!), that give their keepers their flippers when they feed them. There are lions, tigers, bears, bisons, porcupines, mountain goats, lamas and meerkats...

as well as one of the prettiest zoo areas in the world. It has been run for generations by the Hagenbeck family. *Aquarium daily 9am–6pm, zoo March–June, Sept/Oct daily 9am–6pm, July/Aug 9am–7pm, Nov–Feb 9am–4.30pm | combined ticket for park and aquarium (also available individually) 30 euros, children 21 euros | Lokstedter Grenzstr. 2 | tel. 040 5 30 03 30 | www.hagenbeck.de | U 2 Hagenbecks Tierpark*

### INSELPARK WILHELMSBURG
(149 E6) (*0*)

The ideal legacy of an International Garden Show is that it can also be reused – e.g. since the 1973 IGA in *Planten un Blomen* there are some fantastic playgrounds. For the 2013 IGS, at the Inselpark in Wilhelmsburg *(entrance at Neuenfelder Straße | inselpark.hamburg | S 3, 31 Wilhelmsburg)* a genuine play paradise was created. At the playground *Geheimnisvolle Insel* there is a giant slide, in summer children aged above 6 yrs. can climb in the tree-tops of the *Hochseilgarten (April–Oct Fri–Sun, Mon–Sun during holidays | hanserock.de)*. In winter, the *Nordwandhalle* is open with its massive indoor climbing wall and boulders *(daily from 10am | nordwandhalle.*

## The perfect city for families: Hamburg is ideal for a short outing with the children: animals, boats, parks, museums and the theatre

de). Teenies prefer the free skating rink (professional standard) and right in the centre of the park is the *Willi Villa (April–Oct | willivilla.de)* offering pizza, cakes, as well as canoes and SUP for hire.

### JUNGES SCHAUSPIELHAUS
(143 D4) (*Ø H6*)

It's worth making the trip to Ottensen for the truly fabulous plays for kids and young people: up to date and exciting! Tickets 7.50–13 euros. *Gaußstr. 190 | tel. 040 24 87 13 | metro bus 2 Gaußstraße*

### MUSEUMS

All state museums are INSIDER TIP free of charge for children under 18. And all museums offer special children's activities. Contact point is the *Museum Information Service (tel. 040 4 28 13 10 | www.museumsdienst-hamburg.de)*. Fun for children, and inexpensive too, is the customs museum *Zollmuseum (133 D5) (Ø M7) (Tue–Sun 10am–5pm | admission 2 euros, free of charge for children under 17 | Alter Wan-*

drahm 16 | www.museum.zoll.de | U 1 Meß-berg)* in the Speicherstadt. The University's zoological collection, with its array of stuffed animals, ● *Zoologische Sammlung (144 B2) (Ø L5) (Tue–Sun 10am–5pm | Martin-Luther-King-Platz 3 | www.cenak.uni-hamburg.de/en | metro bus 4, 5 Grindelhof)* is free of charge. Here you can also see INSIDER TIP a walrus named Antje, familiar to many Germans from TV.

### WILLKOMMHÖFT (150 B3) (*Ø O*)

At the Wedel welcome point ships are greeted or wished 'bon voyage' with music and their national anthem. Retired captains conduct a flag ceremony and record the ship's tonnage, length and land of origin. On the terrace and at the stalls in front you can get anything you like to eat and drink. Afterwards you can take a walk along the Elbe – perfect for the whole family! *Wedel | Schulauer Fährhaus | daily from 9am | www.schulauer-faehrhaus.de | S 1 Wedel, then bus 189 Elbstraße*

# FESTIVALS & EVENTS

The Hanseatics love festivals: the 'Dom' fair on the Heiligengeistfeld (three times a year), the equestrian event in Klein Flottbek and the many neighbourhood parties, like the *Altonale* in Ottensen or similar ones in St Georg, Eimsbüttel and Winterhude (dates: *hamburg. com/explore/events*).

FESTIVALS

### APRIL/MAY

*Marathon:* for amateurs and professionals. *www.haspa-marathon-hamburg.de/en*
*Long night of museums:* museums open late into the night, free shuttle buses. *www.langenachtdermuseen-hamburg.de*
*Renewable Literature Festival:* author-initiated alternative event in protest of atomic energy. Now, more than 40 artists read over seven days – without a fee, free admission. *www.lesen-ohne-atomstrom.de*
★ *Port anniversary* (early May): huge party along the landing piers with tall ships' parade and 'tug ballet'. *hamburg. com/port-anniversary*

### MAY/JUNE

*Japanese Cherry Blossom Festival:* amazing fireworks around the Alster lake

INSIDER TIP *Elbjazz Festival:* jazz with top musicians in and around the harbour and at the Elbphilharmonie. *www. elbjazz.de/en*
*German Spring Derby Klein Flottbek:* one of the most famous Derbys in the world. *Derbypark | www.engarde.de*

### JUNE/JULY

*Jungle Nights at Hagenbeck:* a zoo becomes a jungle – on several Saturdays. *Lokstedter Grenzstr. 2 | tel. 040 5 30 03 30*
*Altonale:* three weeks of art and culture: at the district fair in Altona. *www.altonale.de*
*Derby week:* fast racehorses and splendid hats in Hamburg Horn. *Rennbahnstr. 96 | www.galopp-hamburg.de/node/33*
*Hamburg Ballet Days:* John Neumeier's ballet never fails to excite. *Staatsoper | www.hamburgballett.de/en*
*Schlagermove:* The music floats of the 'hit parade', which celebrate the 1970s, go right through St Pauli. *www.schlager move.de*

### JULY/AUGUST

*Hamburg Jazz Open:* open-air jazz in Planten un Blomen. *End of June | www. jazzbuero-hamburg.de*
*Hamburger 'Jedermann':* open-air theatre does 'Everyman' in the Speicher-

## Whether sport, the anniversary of the port or a street party – the Hamburgers always like an excuse to celebrate

stadt; on five weekends. *Auf dem Sande | www.hamburger-jedermann.de*
**Triathlon:** swim, cycle and run in the city. *www.hamburg-triathlon.org*
**Christopher Street Day:** originally just for the LGBT community, now a colourful street festival with parade. *St Georg/ Landungsbrücken | www.hamburg-pride. de/en/home*
**Cyclassics:** cycle race for professionals and amateurs. *www.hamburg.de/cyclassics*
**Dockville Festival:** three-day music and art spectacle in Wilhelmsburg. *S 1, 31 Wilhelmsburg | www.msdockville.de*
**Alstervergnügen:** stalls with food and drink, music and amateur dramatics all around the Binnenalster lake. *www.hamburg.de/alstervergnuegen*

### SEPTEMBER/OCTOBER
**Harbour Front Literature Festival:** northern Germany's biggest literature festival with fabulous venues around the harbour, e.g. on 'MS Stubnitz' and 'Cap San Diego'. *www.harbourfront-hamburg.com*

**Night of the Churches:** more than 100 churches open their doors 7pm–midnight, offering services, music, art and literature. *www.ndkh.de*
**Reeperbahnfestival:** Kiez district's music clubs really rock. *End Sept | www.reeperbahnfestival.com/en*
**Hamburg International Film Festival:** a must for film buffs. *www.filmfesthamburg.de/en*

### NOVEMBER/DECEMBER
**China Time:** every two years (2018, 2020 etc.) offering a good cultural programme from and about China. *www.chinatime.hamburg.de/englisch*
**Markt der Völker:** Christmas market in the MARKK Museum am Rothenbaum with presents from around the world.
**Weihnachtsmarkt:** Christmas market on the town hall square, fairy-tale boats for the children are at Jungfernstieg.
**Silvesterfeuerwerk**: New Year's fireworks at the harbour; around midnight the biggest party is at the St-Pauli-landing piers.

# LINKS, BLOGS, APPS & MORE

**LINKS & BLOGS**

www.hamburg.com Hamburg's official tourism website, providing information on accommodation, culture, shopping, public transport, car rental, restaurants, music and sports events, museums and other attractions, as well as living in Hamburg. Includes videos

www.germany.travel/en German tourism website, ideal for those wanting to explore the country further

theater-hamburg.org All Hamburg's theatres at a single (interactive) glance: concert halls like the Laeiszhalle and Elbphilharmonie also feature. The

integrated map is also useful – you instantly know how far to go to the premiere show

www.hvv.de/en all the information you need about public transport in Hamburg, plus bookings and tickets

www.hempels-musictour.com/en Stefanie Hempel is the originator of the musical Beatles-Tour in Hamburg. Follow her and her ukelele in the tracks of the Fab Four across the famous red light district of St Pauli

www.expat-blog.com/en/directory/europe/germany/hamburg there is a contingent of expatriate Brits, Americans and others in Hamburg. Pictures, classified ads and a very lively forum. If you need specific information, then best to ask someone who lives there

www.toytowngermany.com is the best online forum for expats in Germany and the topics of discussion include local news, reviews, relocation issues as well as legal and financial advice. The forum also organises a number of live social events

www.internations.org/hamburg-expats a great forum for people intending to stay longer in the city, or those just getting established

www.spottedbylocals.com/hamburg some really useful tips and suggestions from locals across a broad range of themes of interest to the visitor, from restaurants to music venues and relaxation to shopping www.couchsurfing.org describes itself as the largest traveller community. You don't have to sign up to find profiles of travellers or locals. Click 'Browse People' and then enter 'Hamburg' in the search field

www.airbnb.com the popular site for travellers who prefer to stay in private accommodation offered by locals

**VIDEOS & MUSIC**

www.360cities.net the 360° panoramic photos give an all-round view of top sights. Check out the rotating views of the Speicherstadt by night, the view from the tower of St Michael's Church, the town hall square and many other attractions

www.youtube.com search for any topic you like such as 'Fischmarkt', 'Hafencity' or 'Reeperbahn' to get revealing insights into the real Hamburg

www.miniatur-wunderland.com the best videos from Miniatur-Wunderland, Hamburg's most visited attraction

**APPS**

Hamburg at a Glance: Sights, Tips & Tours produced by the Hamburg Tourist Board. Hamburg's most exciting sights at a glance

TripAdvisor all the usual TripAdvisor information and booking facilities for your tablet or mobile

Hamburg Map & Walks this handy app has detailed tour routes, is ideal to use to explore the city at your own pace and aims to make you feel as though you are being taken around by a local guide

# TRAVEL TIPS

## ARRIVAL

Along the north-south axis via the A7 motorway (Flensburg-Hanover/Kassel); from the east and west via the A1 (Lübeck/Bremen); from Berlin via the A24 and from Heide/Husum via the A23. There are often traffic jams on the A7 around the Elbtunnel during rush hour. For information on public parking see: *english.hamburg.de/1-arrival-in-hamburg-np*

Hamburg has four intercity stations: Hauptbahnhof (with connections to all underground and suburban trains), Dammtor (CCH), Altona and Harburg. ICEs link Hamburg with all major German cities. *www.bahn.com/en/view/index.shtml*

Hamburg International Airport (HAM), since 2016 named 'Helmut Schmidt', is in the north of the city at Fuhlsbüttel. Travel by public transport to the city centre is easy: the S1 leaves the airport (directly under the terminals) every 10 min and it takes just 25 min to Hauptbahnhof. There are four bus services and a night bus that leave the Airport Plaza for various U-Bahn stations. Depending on the destination, a taxi into the city takes 20–40 min and costs from 30 euros. Airport Office: *tel. 040 5 07 50 | hamburg-airport.de/en*

## BOAT EXCURSIONS

At the landing stages and at the Überseebrücke you can pay cash at the kiosk for boat trips to the canals, or on larger vessels to the container terminal. The tour operators are easy to find as most of them shout the announcements and they offer similar prices. Genuine classics are the ● Alster round tours. The white boats stop e.g. at the Jungfernstieg for the *Alster Kreuzfahrt*, which you can hop off on the way *(April–3 Oct | jetty No. 2, day ticket 15 euros)*, or *Dämmertörn (May–3 Oct | 21 euros)* or for a *Winterliche Kreuzfahrt (Nov–March | 15 euros)*. Check the family discount. *tel. 040 3 57 42 40 | alstertouristik.de/English/home.html?*

## RESPONSIBLE TRAVEL

It doesn't take a lot to be environmentally friendly whilst travelling. Don't just think about your carbon footprint whilst flying to and from your holiday destination but also about how you can protect nature and culture abroad. As a tourist it is especially important to respect nature, look out for local products, cycle instead of driving, save water and much more. If you would like to find out more about eco-tourism, please visit: *www.ecotourism.org*

## EMERGENCIES

Police: *tel. 110*; fire brigade/ambulance: *tel. 112*; medical emergency and duty chemist: *tel. 040 22 80 22 (24-hr service)*; emergency doctor's surgery: *Stresemannstr. 54 | Mon/Tue, Thu/Fri 7pm–midnight, Wed 1pm–midnight, Sat/Sun 7am–midnight*; emergency dental service: *tel. 01805 05 05 18 (*)*

## INFORMATION

**HAMBURG TOURISM**
*Postfach 102 249 | 20 015 Hamburg |*

# From arrival to weather

**Your holiday from start to finish: the most important addresses and information for your Hamburg trip**

*hotline +49 (0)40 30 05 13 00 or tel. +49 (0)40 68 99 98 99 (Mon–Sat 9am–7pm) | www.hamburg-travel.com*

**TOURIST INFORMATION**
*– Railway station (exit Kirchenallee) | Mon–Sat 9am–7pm, Sun 10am–6pm*
*– Landungsbrücken (between piers 4 and 5) | Sun–Wed 9am–6pm, Thu–Sat 9am–7pm*
*– Airport (Airport Plaza, arrivals area) | daily 6.30am–11pm*

## PUBLIC TRANSPORT

Single, day and group tickets (also valid for the Hadag Elbe ferries) from Hamburg's public transport authority (HVV) are available from vending machines; children under 6 years of age travel free. At weekends and on public holidays, important bus routes and the S- and U-Bahn lines run around the clock. In addition to covering public transport, the *Hamburg Card* (for 1, 3 or 5 days) allows discounts on admission fees to museums, on theatre tickets, in certain restaurants and on sightseeing tours of the city, port and Alster: day passes (1 adult/3 children) 9.90 euros, group tickets (up to 5 people) 18.50 euros, three-day ticket 25.50 euros (groups 44.50 euros). The *Hamburg Card plus Region* is valid in the whole of the wider HVV area, e.g. to Stade or Bad Segeberg, and includes more than 130 reductions at tourist sights and in shops (day pass for 1 adult/3 children) 21.50 euros; groups up to 5 people 34.90 euros; 3-day pass 58.50 euros/89.50 euros. Available from all HVV service points, the Tourist Information Office, and online at *hamburg-travel. com*. HVV timetable information: *tel. 040 194 49 | hvv.de/en/index.php*

## CURRENCY CONVERTER

| £ | € | € | £ |
|---|---|---|---|
| 1 | 1.10 | 1 | 0.90 |
| 3 | 3.30 | 3 | 2.70 |
| 5 | 5.50 | 5 | 4.50 |
| 13 | 14.30 | 13 | 11.70 |
| 40 | 44 | 40 | 36 |
| 75 | 82.50 | 75 | 67.50 |
| 120 | 132 | 120 | 108 |
| 250 | 275 | 250 | 225 |
| 500 | 550 | 500 | 450 |

| $ | € | € | $ |
|---|---|---|---|
| 1 | 0.80 | 1 | 1.25 |
| 3 | 2.40 | 3 | 3.75 |
| 5 | 4.00 | 5 | 6.25 |
| 13 | 10.40 | 13 | 16.25 |
| 40 | 32 | 40 | 50 |
| 75 | 60 | 75 | 93.75 |
| 120 | 96 | 120 | 250 |
| 250 | 200 | 250 | 312.50 |
| 500 | 400 | 500 | 625 |

For current exchange rates see www.xe.com

## BUDGETING

| | |
|---|---|
| Cappuccino | £2.50/$3.50 |
| | *at a café* |
| Musical | £68–89/$94–123 |
| | *medium price category* |
| Wine | from £4/$5.50 |
| | *per glass at a bar* |
| Pizza | from £7/$10 |
| | *at a restaurant* |
| Boat trip | approx. £16–18/$22–25 |
| | *for a harbour round trip* |
| Bus ride | £2.60/$3.60 |
| | *for a single journey* |

## SIGHTSEEING TOURS

Most buses start from the Hauptbahn-hof, although you can hop on and off. A unique experience is the ● *Hafencity Riverbus (April–Oct 10am–5.15pm, Nov–March 10am–3pm, every 90 min | 29.50 euros | Brooktorkai 16 | tel. 040 76 75 75 00 | hafencityriverbus.de)*. This specially built amphibious bus also floats on the water in Rothenburgsort after a mini city tour (not suitable for children aged under 5 yrs). You can see the port and its ships on the 3-hour INSIDER TIP 'Trip of the Giants' (Gigantentour) laid on by *Jasperreisen (Sat/ Sun, April–Oct also Wed, Fri, May–Sept also Tue | departs U-Bahn Überseequartier, Hafencity | 34 euros | booking and ID card essential | tel. 040 22 71 06 10)*.
*Bicycle-rickshaws:* young cyclists will pedal you around the city. *Trimotion Hamburg | April–Oct | from 6 euros | tel. 0162 108 90 20; Pedalotours Hamburg | tel. 0177 7 36 70 42 | all year | from 6 euros*

## SPORTS

### CYCLING

Bicycles can be taken on the HVV free of charge – at any time of the day during school summer holidays; otherwise not before 9am or between 4pm–6pm, Mon–Fri. The bright red ● City Bikes *(www.stadtradhamburg.de)* are a good way of getting from A to B. There are 207 rental points, most of them at railway and subway stations. The initial payment of 5 euros includes a travel 'credit'; the first 30 min are free and each minute after that is charged at 8 cents. Payment can be made at each terminal with an EC card, a credit/debit card or by phone. Information: *StadtRAD Hamburg | tel. 040 822 188 100. Hamburg-Radtour (meeting point Dammtor | tel. 040 81 99 22 39 | www.hamburg-radtour.de)* is one of several

companies offering guided tours by bike. With the e-bikes from the cycle hire at *Erfahre Hamburg (9 euros/4 hrs, 15 euros/ day | Vorsetzen 50 | tel. 040 74 20 36 02 | erfahre.com)* you can happily cycle as far as Blankenese.

### FITNESS & SPA

The *Meridian Spa* in Hoheluft *is popular (daily | from 20 euros | Quickbornstr. 26 | tel. 040 65 89 13 43 | meridianspa.de)* as well as the ● *Kaifu-Sole* sauna *(daily | 21 euros | Hohe Weide 15 | tel. 040 18 88 90 | baederland.de)*. In the beautifully restored building you can bathe in the saltwater, relax in two saunas, book a massage and use the swimming pool.

### PADDLING & ROWING

Many boat hires rent canoes and rowing boats (April–Oct). Note: The further away they are located from the part of the Alster lake called the Außenalster the lower the price. Boat rental from 9.50 euros/hr.
– Boat rental *Dornheim (Kaemmerufer 25 | tel. 040 279 41 84)*
– Boat rental on the *Liebesinsel* in the Stadtpark (city park) *(Südring 5a | tel. 040 27 34 16)*

### SAILING ●

Lessons and yacht rental on the Alster:
– *Segelschule Pieper (Atlanticsteg | tel. 040 24 75 78 | segelschule-pieper.de)*
– *Käpt'n Prüsse (An der Alster 47a | Gurlittinsel | tel. 040 2 80 31 31 | pruesse.de)*

### SWIMMING

The renovated *Holthusenbad (Goernestr. 21 | U 1, 3 Kellinghusenstraße)* in Eppendorf has many bathing options, e.g. wave pool, outdoor pool and sauna. Ask for the romantic INSIDER TIP Candlelight Spa, then you can swim by candlelight. Close to the centre in St Georg is the *Alsterschwimmhalle (Ifflandstr. 21 | U 1, 3 Lübecker*

*Straße)* with its 50-m/164-ft pool. In summer the *natural pool Naturbad Stadtparksee (Südring 5b | U 3 Saarlandstraße)* and the *Finkenwerder Open Air Pool (Finkenwerder Finksweg 82 | HADAG ferries 62, 64 Finkenwerder Landungsbrücke)*, where you can watch the ships while you swim, are pure bliss. For all pools: *tel. 040 18 88 90*

## TAXI

Das Taxi: *tel. 040 22 11 22*; Hansa Funktaxi: *tel. 040 211211*; Taxi Hamburg: *tel. 040 66 66 66*; ⊙ prima clima mobil: *tel. 040 2115 22* – this taxi firm only uses low-emission vehicles.

## THEATRE/CONCERT TICKETS

– *Konzertkasse Gerdes (Rothenbaumchaussee 77 | tel. 040 45 03 50 60),* good advice on classical concerts.
– *Konzertkasse Hauptbahnhof (Spitaler Str. exit | tel. 040 32 87 38 54)*

– *Konzertkasse Schanze (Schanzenstr. 5 | tel. 040 38 65 51 95)*

## WALKING/BOAT TOURS

*Stattreisen Hamburg e. V. (tel. 040 87 08 01 00 | www.stattreisen-hamburg.de)* offers different tours like the 'Harbour for Children' and boat tours. The *Rosinenfischer (tel. 040 36 09 19 83 | rosinenfischer.de)* tour of the Speicherstadt and Hafencity, and depending on the theme there is chocolate, coffee beans and other delicacies to sample; e-bike-tours are also available. 'Sensory' tours Sat/Sun year-round *(19 euros). Rock 'n' Roll live (April–Nov Sat 6pm | 2.5hrs | from 28.50 euros | from U-Bahn Feldstr. | tel. 040 30 03 37 90 | www.hemp els-musictour.de/en/):* on her Beatles Tour through St Pauli the musician Stefanie Hempel relates some amazing stories about the Fab Four, sings and plays the best songs on her ukulele and closes the tour with a concert in the St Pauli Museum.

# WEATHER IN HAMBURG

| | Jan | Feb | March | April | May | June | July | Aug | Sept | Oct | Nov | Dec |
|---|---|---|---|---|---|---|---|---|---|---|---|---|
| Daytime temperatures in °C/°F | 2/36 | 3/37 | 8/46 | 13/55 | 18/64 | 22/72 | 23/73 | 23/73 | 19/66 | 13/55 | 7/45 | 4/39 |
| Nighttime temperatures in °C/°F | –3/27 | –3/27 | 0/32 | 3/37 | 7/45 | 11/52 | 13/55 | 13/55 | 10/50 | 6/43 | 2/36 | –1/30 |
| ☀ Sunshine hours/day | 2 | 2 | 4 | 6 | 8 | 8 | 7 | 6 | 6 | 2 | 2 | 1 |
| ☂ Precipitation days/month | 12 | 10 | 8 | 10 | 10 | 10 | 12 | 11 | 10 | 10 | 11 | 11 |

# USEFUL PHRASES GERMAN

## PRONUNCIATION

We have provided a simple pronunciation aid for the german words
(see the square brackets). Note the following:

| | |
|---|---|
| ch | usually like ch in Scottish 'loch', shown here as [kh] |
| g | hard as in 'get' |
| ß | is a double s |
| ä | like the vowel in 'fair' or 'bear' |
| ö | a little like er as in 'her' |
| ü | is spoken as ee with rounded lips, like the French 'tu' |
| ie | is ee as in 'fee', but ei is like 'height', shown here as [ei] |
| ' | stress on the following syllable |

### IN BRIEF

| | |
|---|---|
| Yes/No/Maybe | Ja [yah]/Nein [nein]/Vielleicht [fee'leikht] |
| Please/Thank you | Bitte ['bi-te]/Danke ['dan-ke] |
| Sorry | Entschuldigung [ent'shul-di-ge] |
| Excuse me, please | Entschuldigen Sie [ent'shul-di-gen zee] |
| May I ...?/ Pardon? | Darf ich ...? [darf ikh]/Wie bitte? [vee 'bi-te] |
| I would like to .../ have you got ...? | Ich möchte ... [ikh 'merkh-te]/ Haben Sie ...? ['hab-en zee] |
| How much is ...? | Wie viel kostet ...? [vee-feel 'koss-tet] |
| I (don't) like this | Das gefällt mir/nicht [das ge-'felt meer/nikht] |
| good/bad | gut/schlecht [goot/shlekht] |
| broken/doesn't work | kaputt [ka-'put]/funktioniert nicht/ funk-tsion-'eert nikht] |
| (too) much/little | (zu) viel/wenig [tsoo feel/'vay-nikh] |
| Help!/Attention!/ Caution! | Hilfe! ['hil-fe]/Achtung! [akh-'tung]/ Vorsicht! ['for-sikht] |
| ambulance | Krankenwagen ['kran-ken-vaa-gen]/ Notarzt ['note-aatst] |
| police/fire brigade | Polizei [pol-i-'tsei]/Feuerwehr ['foy-er-vayr] |
| danger/dangerous | Gefahr [ge-'far]/gefährlich [ge-'fair-likh] |

### GREETINGS, FAREWELL

| | |
|---|---|
| Good morning!/after-noon!/evening!/night! | Gute(n) Morgen ['goo-ten 'mor-gen]/Tag [taag]/ Abend ['aa-bent]/Nacht [nakht] |
| Hello!/goodbye! | Hallo! ['ha-llo]/Auf Wiedersehen [owf 'vee-der-zayn] |

# Sprichst du Deutsch?

'Do you speak German?' This guide will help you to
say the basic words and phrases in German.

| | |
|---|---|
| See you! | Tschüss [chüss] |
| My name is ... | Ich heiße ... [ikh 'hei-sse] |
| What's your name? | Wie heißt Du [vee heist doo]/ heißen Sie? ['heiss-en zee] |
| I'm from ... | Ich komme aus ... [ikh 'ko-mme ows] |

## DATE & TIME

| | |
|---|---|
| Monday/Tuesday | Montag ['moan-tag]/Dienstag ['deens-tag] |
| Wednesday/Thursday | Mittwoch ['mit-vokh]/Donnerstag ['don-ers-tag] |
| Friday/Saturday | Freitag ['frei-tag]/Samstag ['zams-tag] |
| Sunday/holiday | Sonntag ['zon-tag]/Feiertag ['fire-tag] |
| today/tomorrow/ yesterday | heute ['hoy-te]/morgen ['mor-gen]/ gestern ['gess-tern] |
| hour/minute | Stunde ['shtun-de]/Minute [min-'oo-te] |
| day/night/week | Tag [tag]/Nacht [nakht]/Woche ['vo-khe] |
| What time is it? | Wie viel Uhr ist es? ['vee-feel oor ist es] |
| It's three o'clock | Es ist drei Uhr [ez ist drei oor] |

## TRAVEL

| | |
|---|---|
| open/closed | offen ['off-en]/geschlossen [ge-'shloss-en] |
| entrance (vehicles) | Zufahrt ['tsoo-faat] |
| entrance/exit | Eingang ['ein-gang]/Ausgang ['ows-gang] |
| arrival/departure (flight) | Ankunft ['an-kunft]/Abflug ['ap-floog] |
| toilets/restrooms / ladies/gentlemen | Toiletten [twa-'let-en]/ Damen ['daa-men]/Herren ['her-en] |
| (no) drinking water | (kein) Trinkwasser [(kein) 'trink-vass-er] |
| Where is ...?/Where are ...? | Wo ist ...? [vo ist]/Wo sind ...? [vo zint] |
| left/right | links [links]/rechts [rekhts] |
| straight ahead/back | geradeaus [ge-raa-de-'ows]/zurück [tsoo-'rük] |
| close/far | nah [naa]/weit [veit] |
| taxi/cab | Taxi ['tak-si] |
| bus stop/ cab stand | Bushaltestelle [bus-hal-te-'shtell-e]/ Taxistand ['tak-si- shtant] |
| parking lot/parking garage | Parkplatz ['park-plats]/Parkhaus ['park-hows] |
| street map/map | Stadtplan ['shtat-plan]/Landkarte ['lant-kaa-te] |
| airport/train station | Flughafen ['floog-ha-fen]/ Bahnhof ['baan-hoaf] |
| schedule/ticket | Fahrplan ['faa-plan]/Fahrschein ['faa-shein] |
| I would like to rent ... | Ich möchte ... mieten [ikh 'mer-khte ... 'mee-ten] |
| a car/a bicycle | ein Auto [ein 'ow-to]/ein Fahrrad [ein 'faa-raat] |
| a motorhome/RV | ein Wohnmobil [ein 'vone-mo-beel] |
| a boat | ein Boot [ein 'boat] |

| petrol/gas station | Tankstelle ['tank-shtell-e] |
| petrol/gas / diesel | Benzin [ben-'tseen]/Diesel ['dee-zel] |
| breakdown/repair shop | Panne ['pan-e]/Werkstatt ['verk-shtat] |

## FOOD & DRINK

| Could you please book a table for tonight for four? | Reservieren Sie uns bitte für heute Abend einen Tisch für vier Personen [rez-er-'vee-ren zee uns 'bi-te für 'hoy-te 'aa-bent 'ein-en tish für feer pair-'zo-nen] |
| The menu, please | Die Speisekarte, bitte [dee 'shpei-ze-kaa-te 'bi-te] |
| Could I please have ...? | Könnte ich ... haben? ['kern-te ihk ... 'haa-ben] |
| with/without ice/ sparkling | mit [mit]/ohne Eis ['oh-ne eis]/ Kohlensäure ['koh-len-zoy-re] |
| vegetarian/allergy | Vegetarier(in) [veg-e-'taa-ree-er]/Allergie [al-air-'gee] |
| May I have the bill, please? | Ich möchte zahlen, bitte [ikh 'merkh-te 'tsaa-len 'bi-te] |

## SHOPPING

| Where can I find...? | Wo finde ich ...? [vo 'fin-de ikh] |
| I'd like .../I'm looking for ... | Ich möchte ... [ikh 'merkh-te]/Ich suche ... [ikh 'zoo-khe] |
| pharmacy/chemist | Apotheke [a-po-'tay-ke]/Drogerie [dro-ge-'ree] |
| shopping centre | Einkaufszentrum [ein-kowfs-'tsen-trum] |
| expensive/cheap/price | teuer ['toy-er]/billig ['bil-ig]/Preis [preis] |
| more/less | mehr [mayr]/weniger ['vay-ni-ger] |
| organically grown | aus biologischem Anbau [ows bee-o-'lo-gish-em 'an-bow] |

## ACCOMMODATION

| I have booked a room | Ich habe ein Zimmer reserviert [ikh 'haa-be ein 'tsi-me rez-erv-'eert] |
| Do you have any ... left? | Haben Sie noch ... ['haa-ben zee nokh] |
| single room | Einzelzimmer ['ein-tsel-tsi-mer] |
| double room | Doppelzimmer ['dop-el-tsi-mer] |
| breakfast/half board | Frühstück ['frü-shtük]/Halbpension ['halp-pen-si-ohn] |
| full board | Vollpension ['foll-pen-si-ohn] |
| shower/sit-down bath | Dusche ['doo-she]/Bad [baat] |
| balcony/terrasse | Balkon [bal-'kohn]/Terrasse [te-'rass-e] |
| key/room card | Schlüssel ['shlü-sel]/Zimmerkarte ['tsi-mer-kaa-te] |
| luggage/suitcase | Gepäck [ge-'pek]/Koffer ['koff-er]/Tasche ['ta-she] |

## BANKS, MONEY & CREDIT CARDS

| bank/ATM | Bank/Geldautomat [bank/'gelt-ow-to-maat] |
| pin code | Geheimzahl [ge-'heim-tsaal] |
| I'd like to change ... | Ich möchte ... wechseln [ikh 'merkh-te ... 'vek-seln] |

| | |
|---|---|
| cash/credit card | bar [bar]/Kreditkarte [kre-'dit-kaa-te] |
| bill/coin | Banknote ['bank-noh-te]/Münze ['mün-tse] |

## HEALTH

| | |
|---|---|
| doctor/dentist/ | Arzt [aatst]/Zahnarzt ['tsaan-aatst]/ |
| paediatrician | Kinderarzt ['kin-der-aatst] |
| hospital/ | Krankenhaus ['kran-ken-hows]/ |
| emergency clinic | Notfallpraxis ['note-fal-prak-sis] |
| fever/pain | Fieber ['fee-ber]/Schmerzen ['shmer-tsen] |
| diarrhoea/nausea | Durchfall ['doorkh-fal]/Übelkeit ['ü-bel-keit] |
| inflamed/injured | entzündet [ent-'tsün-det]/verletzt [fer-'letst] |
| prescription | Rezept [re-'tsept] |
| pain reliever/tablet | Schmerzmittel ['shmerts-mit-el]/Tablette [ta-'blet-e] |

## POST, TELECOMMUNICATIONS & MEDIA

| | |
|---|---|
| stamp/letter | Briefmarke ['brief-maa-ke]/Brief [brief] |
| postcard | Postkarte ['posst-kaa-te] |
| I'm looking for a prepaid | Ich suche eine Prepaid-Karte für mein Handy [ikh |
| card for my mobile | 'zoo-khe 'ei-ne 'pre-paid-kaa-te für mein 'hen-dee] |
| Do I need a special | Brauche ich eine spezielle Vorwahl? |
| area code? | ['brow-khe ikh 'ei-ne shpets-ee-'ell-e 'fore-vaal] |
| Where can I find internet | Wo finde ich einen Internetzugang? |
| access? | [vo 'fin-de ikh 'ei-nen 'in-ter-net-tsoo-gang] |
| socket/adapter/ | Steckdose ['shtek-doh-ze]/Adapter [a-'dap-te]/ |
| charger/wi-fi | Ladegerät ['laa-de-ge-rayt]/WLAN ['vay-laan] |

## LEISURE, SPORTS & BEACH

| | |
|---|---|
| bike/scooter rental | Fahrrad-['faa-raat]/Mofa-Verleih ['mo-fa fer-lei] |
| rental shop | Vermietung [fer-'mee-tung] |
| lesson | Übungsstunde ['ü-bungs-shtun-de] |

## NUMBERS

| | | |
|---|---|---|
| 0 null [null] | 10 zehn [tsayn] | 20 zwanzig ['tsvantsikh] |
| 1 eins [eins] | 11 elf [elf] | 50 fünfzig ['fünf-tsikh] |
| 2 zwei [tsvei] | 12 zwölf [tsvölf] | 100 (ein) hundert ['hun-dert] |
| 3 drei [drei] | 13 dreizehn [' dreitsayn] | 200 zwei hundert [tsvei 'hun-dert] |
| 4 vier [feer] | 14 vierzehn ['feertsayn] | 1000 (ein) tausend ['tow-zent] |
| 5 fünf [fünf] | 15 fünfzehn ['fünftsayn] | 2000 zwei tausend [tsvei 'tow-zent] |
| 6 sechs [zex] | 16 sechzehn ['zekhtsayn] | 10 000 zehn tausend [tsayn 'tow-zent] |
| 7 sieben ['zeeben] | 17 siebzehn ['zeebtsayn] | |
| 8 acht [akht] | 18 achtzehn ['akhtsayn] | ½ ein halb [ein halp] |
| 9 neun [noyn] | 19 neunzehn ['noyntsayn] | ¼ ein viertel [ein 'feer-tel] |

# STREET ATLAS

The green line indicates the Discovery Tour 'Hamburg at a glance'
The blue line indicates the other Discovery Tours

All tours are also marked on the pull-out map

Photo: Binnenalster

# Exploring Hamburg

The map on the back cover shows how
the area has been sub-divided

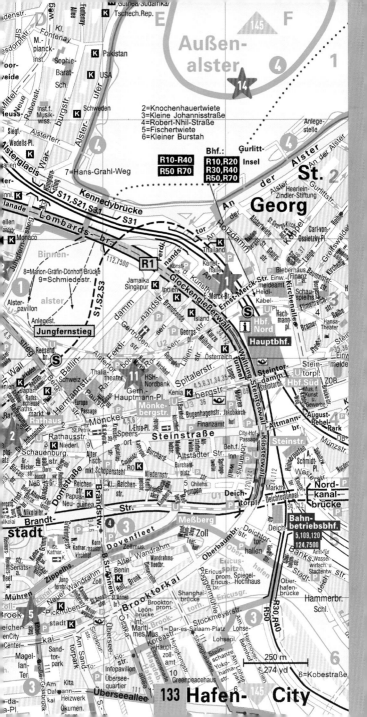

Außen-alster

14

2=Knochenhauertwiete
3=Kleine Johannisstraße
4=Robert-Nhil-Straße
5=Fischertwiete
6=Kleiner Burstah

7=Hans-Grahl-Weg

Bhf.:
| R10-R40 | R10,R20 |
|---------|---------|
| R50 R70 | R30,R40 |
|         | R50,R70 |

Kennedybrücke

St. Georg

Anlege-stelle

8=Manon-Gräfin-Dönhoff-Brücke
9=Schmiedestr.

R1

Jungfernstieg

Hbf. Nord

Hauptbhf.

Steintor

Hbf. Süd

ZOB

Rathaus

Mönckebergstr.

Steinstraße

Nord-kanal-brücke

Brandt-stadt

Dovenfleet

Meßberg

Zoll

Bahn-betriebsbhf.

Mühren-brook

Brooktorkai

Hammerbr. Schl.

250 m
274 yd

6=Kobestraße

133 Hafen- City

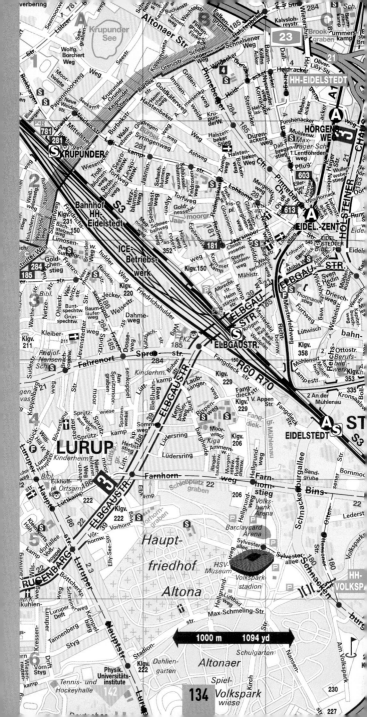

**Hyperboloid-Projektion (Lupeneffekt):** Maßstabsveränderung vom Stadtzentrum zu den Außenbezirken

**Hyperboloid projection (magnifying glass effect):** Change of scale from the inner city to the outlying districts

# NIENDORF

1000 m    1094 yd

*Niendorfer Gehege*

HAGENDEEL

HAGENBECKS TIERPARK

# LOKSTEDT

STELLINGEN

STELLINGEN

Langenfelde

LANGENFELDE

135

GROSS-BORSTEL

Papen-

Nieder-

Nedder-feld

Nedderfeld

SIEMERS

Osterfeld

Anscharhöhe
Stift
St. Anschar

Bei der Lutherbuche

Sottorfallee

Studenten-
wohnhm.

Siebenschön

Brunsberg

Behrkampsweg

Platanenallee

Universitäts-
klinikum-
Hamburg-
Eppendorf
(UKE)

EPPENDORF

SC
Victoria

HOHE-
LUFT

HOHELUFT
OST

HOHELUFT
WEST

EPPENDORF
BAUM

KLOSTERS...

Philipp
Ecador

136

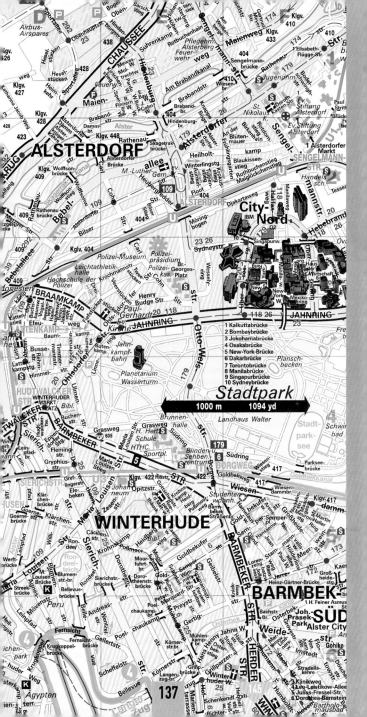

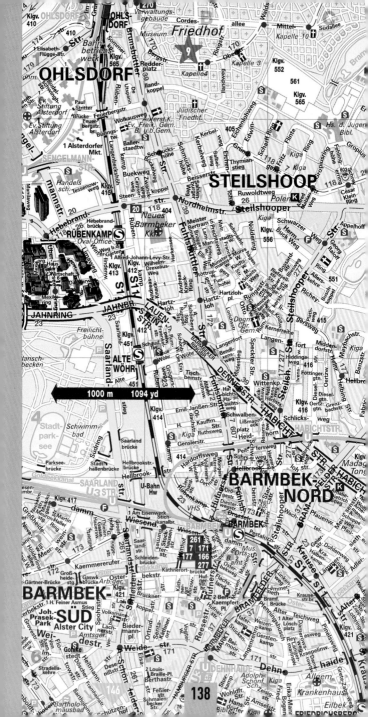

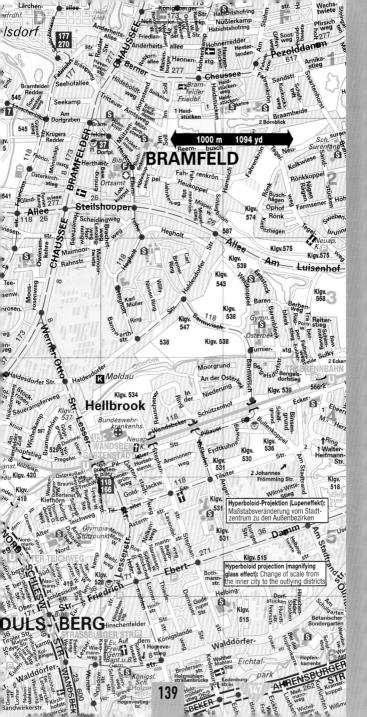

**1000 m    1094 yd**

# BRAMFELD

## Hellbrook

**Hyperboloid-Projektion (Lupeneffekt):**
Maßstabsveränderung vom Stadtzentrum zu den Außenbezirken

**Hyperboloid projection (magnifying
glass effect):** Change of scale from
the inner city to the outlying districts

# DULS-BERG

**139**

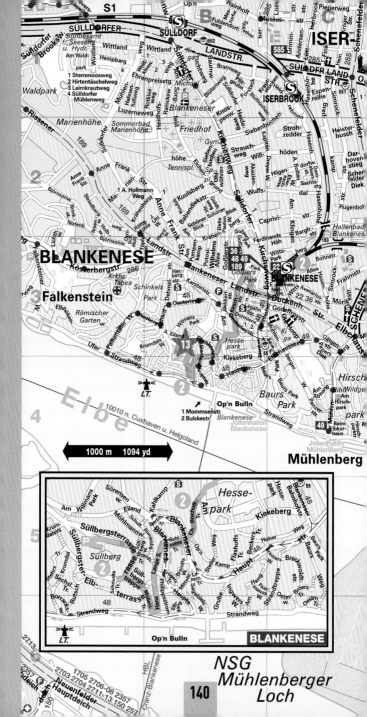

Hyperboloid-Projektion (Lupeneffekt):
Maßstabsveränderung vom Stadtzentrum zu den Außenbezirken

Hyperboloid projection (magnifying glass effect): Change of scale from the inner city to the outlying districts

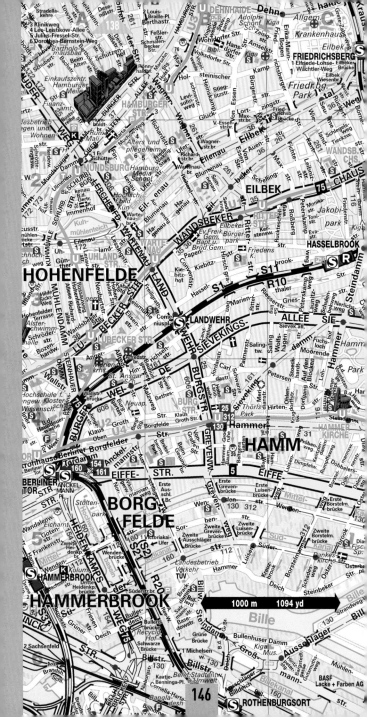

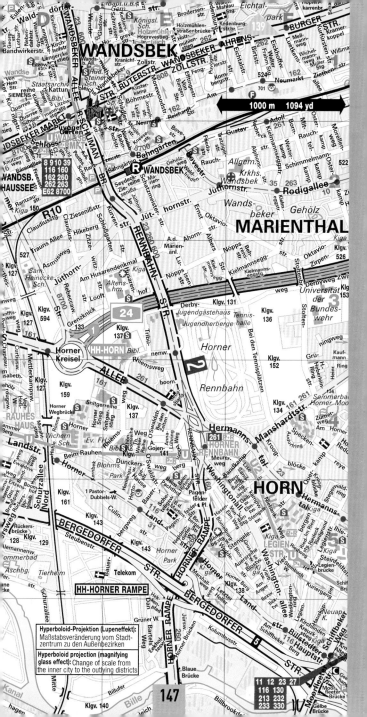

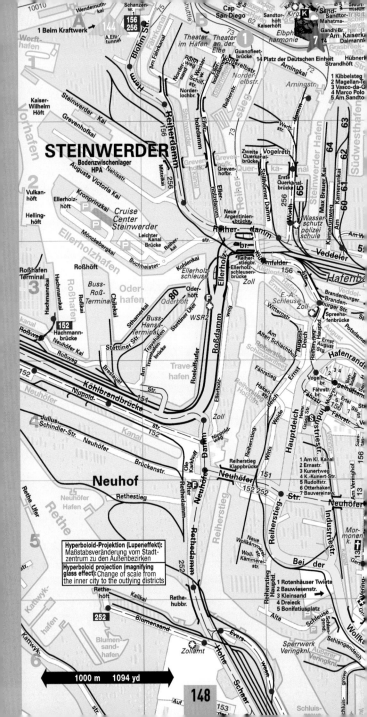

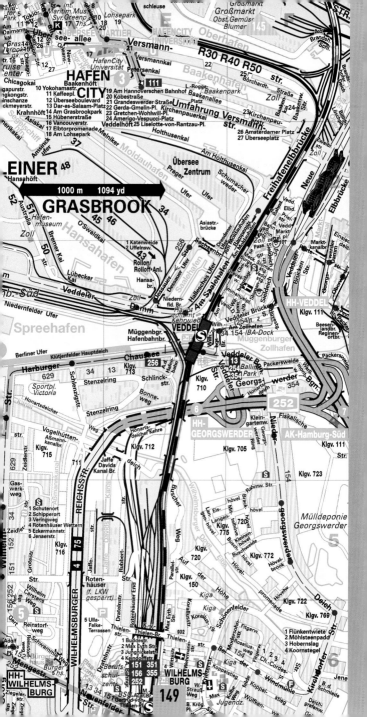

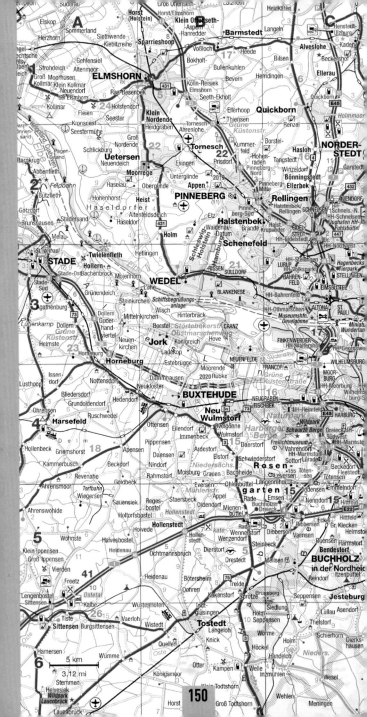

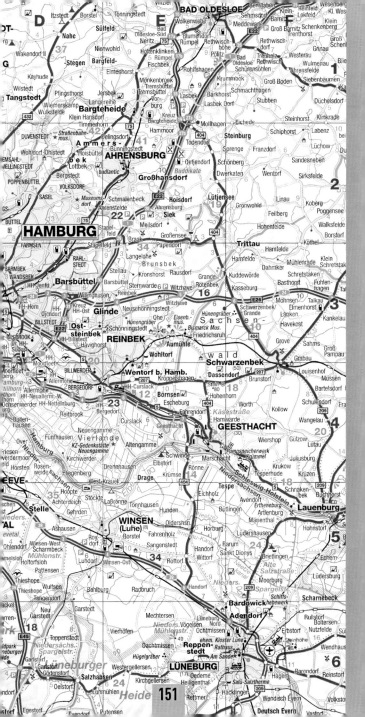

This index lists a selection of the streets and squares shown in the street atlas

# KEY TO STREET ATLAS

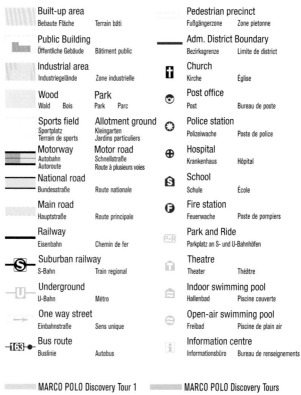

| | | |
|---|---|---|
| Built-up area | | Pedestrian precinct |
| Bebaute Fläche | Terrain bâti | Fußgängerzone / Zone pietonne |
| Public Building | | Adm. District Boundary |
| Öffentliche Gebäude | Bâtiment public | Bezirksgrenze / Limite de district |
| Industrial area | | Church |
| Industriegelände | Zone industrielle | Kirche / Église |
| Wood | Park | Post office |
| Wald  Bois | Park  Parc | Post / Bureau de poste |
| Sports field | Allotment ground | Police station |
| Sportplatz / Terrain de sports | Kleingarten / Jardins particuliers | Polizeiwache / Poste de police |
| Motorway | Motor road | Hospital |
| Autobahn / Autoroute | Schnellstraße / Route à plusieurs voies | Krankenhaus / Hôpital |
| National road | | School |
| Bundesstraße | Route nationale | Schule / École |
| Main road | | Fire station |
| Hauptstraße | Route principale | Feuerwache / Poste de pompiers |
| Railway | | Park and Ride |
| Eisenbahn | Chemin de fer | Parkplatz an S- und U-Bahnhöfen |
| Suburban railway | | Theatre |
| S-Bahn | Train regional | Theater / Théâtre |
| Underground | | Indoor swimming pool |
| U-Bahn | Métro | Hallenbad / Piscine couverte |
| One way street | | Open-air swimming pool |
| Einbahnstraße | Sens unique | Freibad / Piscine de plain air |
| Bus route | | Information centre |
| Buslinie | Autobus | Informationsbüro / Bureau de renseignements |

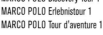

MARCO POLO Discovery Tour 1        MARCO POLO Discovery Tours
MARCO POLO Erlebnistour 1           MARCO POLO Erlebnistouren
MARCO POLO Tour d'aventure 1        MARCO POLO Tours d'aventure

  MARCO POLO Highlight

---

**Hyperboloid-projection (magnifying effect):**
The map projection brings about a change of scale from the city centre to the outlying districts. Consequently the city centre is presented in a more readable form (magnifying glass effect). The black arrows are to estimate distances; the length of each arrow represents 1 km / 0.62 mi.

# MARCO POLO TRAVEL GUIDES

# INDEX

This index lists all sights and destinations plus the names of important streets, places, people and keywords featured in this guide. Numbers in bold indicate a main entry.

# CREDITS

# WRITE TO US

e-mail: info@marcopologuides.co.uk
Did you have a great holiday?
Is there something on your mind?
Whatever it is, let us know!
Whether you want to praise, alert us
to errors or give us a personal tip –
MARCO POLO would be pleased to
hear from you.
We do everything we can to provide the
very latest information for your trip.

Nevertheless, despite all of our authors'
thorough research, errors can creep in.
MARCO POLO does not accept any
liability for this. Please contact us by
e-mail or post.
MARCO POLO Travel Publishing Ltd
Pinewood, Chineham Business Park
Crockford Lane, Chineham
Basingstoke, Hampshire RG24 8AL
United Kingdom

**PICTURE CREDITS**
Cover photograph: Speicherstadt (Getty Images: justhanni)
Photos: Getty Images: A. Cappelli (118/119), DaniloAndjus (3), justhanni (1); A. Honert (1); huber-images: Grä-
fenhain (68 left), H.-P. Merten (37); Laif: D. Eisermann (72/73, 85), G. Haenel (115), B. Jonkmanns (32, 55,
76, 95, 116/117), C. Kerber (18 centre), G. Knechtel (66, 121), H. Meyer (14), J. Modrow (40, 119), D. Schwel-
le (7), Selbach (10, 90/91), F. Siemers (62, 74, 116, 117), G. Theis (69); S. Volk (48); Laif/Le Figaro Magazine:
Martin (5, 17, 31); Look: H. Dressler (112), A. Haug (4 bottom, 47, 107), H. Wohner (56, 120 top); mauritius
images: I. Boelter (12/13, 20/21, 39, 71, 88, 100/101), T. Ebelt (118), Jonna (flap left), Waldkirch (4 top, 23);
mauritius images/imagebroker: Ch. Ohde (92); mauritius images/The Travel Collection: W. Schmitz (80/81);
mauritius images/Westend61: (2, 58), Willing-Holtz (18 top); picture-alliance/dpa: C. Charisius (6), M. Scholz
(19 top); D. Renckhoff (53, 65, 82); vario images/C hromorange (front flap, right, 24/25); vario images/image-
broker (26/27, 120 bottom); vario images/M c Photo (42, 45); vario images/Westend61 (126/127); Visum: M.
Bustamante (18 bottom), B. Euler (60/61); M. von Hessert-Fraatz (8, 19 bottom, 79, 87, 96,98); White Star:
Pasdzior (51); M. Zapf (9, 11, 34, 50, 68 right)

**3rd edition 2019 – fully revised and updated**
Worldwide Distribution: Marco Polo Travel Publishing Ltd, Pinewood, Chineham Business Park, Crockford Lane,
Basingstoke, Hampshire RG24 8AL, United Kingdom. E-mail: sales@marcopolouk.com
© MAIRDUMONT GmbH & Co. KG , Ostfildern
Chief editor: Stefanie Penck; author: Dorothea Heintze; co-author: Katrin Wienefeld; editor: Jochen Schürmann
Programme supervision: Lucas Forst-Gill, Susanne Hanburger, Nikolai Michaelis, Martin Silbermann, Kristin
Wittemann; picture editors: Gabriele Forst, Anja Schlatterer
Cartography street atlas and pull-out map: © MAIRDUMONT, Ostfildern; cover design, p. 1, pull-out map cover:
Karl Anders – Büro für Visual Stories, Hamburg; design inside: milchhof:atelier, Berlin; design p. 2/3, Discovery
Tours: Susan Chaaban Dipl.-Des. (FH)
Translated from German by Tony Halliday, Jane Riester and Suzanne Kirkbright
Editorial office: SAW Communications, Redaktionsbüro Dr. Sabine A. Werner, Mainz: Julia Gilcher, Kristin Smolinna,
Cosima Talhouni, Dr. Sabine A. Werner; prepress: SAW Communications, Mainz, in cooperation with alles mit
Medien, Mainz
Phrase book in cooperation with Ernst Klett Sprachen GmbH, Stuttgart
Editorial by Pons Wörterbücher
All rights reserved. No part of this book may be reproduced, stored in a
retrieval system or transmitted in any form or by any means (electronic,
mechanical, photocopying, recording or otherwise) without prior written
permission. Printed in China

MIX
Paper from
responsible sources
FSC® C124385

## DON'T PARK IN THE WRONG PLACE

For landlubbers the car parks right on the banks of the Elbe, for example at the Fischmarkt in Altona or Övelgönne, may look completely safe and dry. But floods can happen quickly and sometimes unexpectedly, and the police are not always on hand to tow away vehicles. Don't leave your car there for too long unattended, and heed the warnings!

## DO BEHAVE ON THE REEPERBAHN

Of course you want to go to the Reeperbahn – and you should – but try to follow a few written, and unwritten, rules. Don't try the patience of the professional ladies in the side streets; they have a job to do, just like the rest of us. Weapons of all kinds are forbidden and you are not allowed to drink out of glass bottles on the street at the weekend. The police react quickly and show no tolerance.

## DO WATCH OUT

Nowhere is it really dangerous in Hamburg, unless you start trouble at night on the Reeperbahn (known colloquially as the 'Kiez') or around Hansaplatz in St Georg. Be that as it may, Hamburg is a big city and pickpockets are everywhere, particularly in those places where there are jostling crowds, such as the Fischmarkt. Keep an eye on your belongings!

## DON'T LEAVE RUBBISH ON THE BEACHES

On balmy summer evenings, the beaches along the Elbe in Övelgönne and Wittenbergen are full of little fires, portable barbecues and young people strumming guitars. The whole thing is wonderfully romantic – though it's not officially allowed, just tolerated – but please light your fire only where it is allowed and don't leave your rubbish behind!

## DON'T MOAN ABOUT THE WEATHER

Yes, of course the weather could be better. The people of Hamburg know that themselves. But what's the point of moaning about it? A better idea is to take a raincoat and pullover with you and try to be optimistic! Even the lowest-lying, leaden clouds have a silver lining.

## DO BE ALERT WHEN WALKING OR DRIVING

Many strangers to the city have almost had a heart attack when, walking innocently along the pavement, they are suddenly overtaken – within a whisker and without any warning – by a cyclist going at breakneck speed. In Hamburg cyclists are allowed to ride on many pavements and they are often quite inconsiderate. Keep your eyes open when you are driving too: cyclists are allowed to ride down many one-way streets in the opposite direction.